RESET

REFORMATTING YOUR PURPOSE
FOR TOMORROW'S WORLD

by Dr. Jason T. Brooks

Publication Information Page

Unless otherwise notes, Scripture quotations have been taken from the New King James Version. © 1996 by Tyndale House Publishers.

ISBN: 061572812X
ISBN 13: 9780615728124
Library of Congress Control Number: 2012921780

To my bride, Darla, and children, Andrew, Nathanael, and Aleya.

Praise for RESET

"Bravo! Dr. Jason Brooks has ripped the veil away and set free a lost generation—every man and woman alive who feel their life isn't headed in the direction they intended can experience a radical RESET."

> *Ron Loveless, retired Walmart executive/founding CEO of Sam's Club/business consultant*

"RESET has the power to transform your future."

> *Dr. Tom Hill, coauthor of "Chicken Soup for the Entrepreneur's Soul" and cofounder of the Tom Hill Institute*

"Dr. Jason Brooks is a strategist. This book is proof that to revisit the core elements of any corporate or societal success strategy we must focus on the power of our own humanity and purpose. This book is a practical roadmap for individuals as well as organizations to clearly define the desired end result and activate a powerful course to get there that starts today."

> *John Guerra, CEO, Aztec Worldwide Group, LTD. and the United Consumer Coalition, former managing director, AT&T Caribbean, Latin Americas and Mexico.*

"Every blue moon a book appears that changes everything. Once you start reading RESET, you can't stop."

> *Louis Upkins, entrepreneur and author of "Treat Me Like a Customer"*

"After reading Dr. Brooks' book, I too have hit RESET to find my true passion and rewrite my life story. I am certain that I am now on the path to living out my legacy."

Suzanne Leonard, founding CEO, Vanguard Leaders and Legends & Legacy, former executive director for the Global Speed of Trust Practice with Stephen M.R. Covey

"So often we look for missing pieces to find success. RESET proves that the answers we seek might already be there-they are simply not in alignment. A great read."

Brett Blair, president, Sanford Rose Associates – Blair Leadership Group

"Empower your people to empower your business. RESET is the book that should be central to your organizational strategy, because people are central to your strategy."

Steve Hayes, senior partner, The Human Capital Group, Inc.

"RESET asks the right questions. During the process of reading, you not only understand yourself, but also the 'why' behind many of your successes and failures."

Rick Kloete, president and managing partner, The Kloete Group, Inc.

"Dr. Brooks has written the book that unlocks the button many secretly wish to push—RESET! If you have ever thought a "do-over" was in order, now is the time! You can have the life you've always wanted."

Dave Jaworski, COO, The Lifebook Company and first recipient of Bill Gates's Chairman's Award for Excellence

Contents

Spiritual awarness ch, pg 79

Foreword

By Louis Upkins

In life, we all go through different seasons. Some are seasons of great opportunities and success. Others are times of rest and refocus. Still others are times of trial where we are stretched, sometimes beyond what we could have imagined or thought we could endure. Each of these seasons is appointed for different reasons. But in the end, each is a piece of our life puzzle that has created the picture of who we are and the future ahead. In my life, I have faced many times that have required a RESET as I moved from one season to the next. I was blessed to have built an exciting career in the early years of my professional experience. I was living the life every "successful" businessman dreams. High-end experiences, world travel, and collaborating with some of the largest names in a variety of industries, across the board, from large sports and entertainment outlets and personalities to Fortune 500 companies and celebrities were the norm. I was living large and enjoying every minute. But, a sense of change was coming as I began to consider my dreams of marriage and starting a family. I began to realize the having a "successful life" would require getting off the road and preparing for a change in life ahead. Priorities would shift. Clients would change. But I knew that if I were to ever have the marriage, family, and quality relationship with those who would mean the most to me, I needed to change direction. This certainly brought me to a point of needing to prioritize against risk and create a new path that was in alignment with my new focus. I needed a RESET.

This transition to creating greater stability and consistency allowed me to enter into the most important relationship of my life with my wife. She is my heartbeat and has been a continual source of encouragement and support during times of transition. At no time did we experience such a crisis of belief as when I made my next major life shift away from my life as a marketing and branding entrepreneur to devoting all of my attention to developing leaders through the work of my first book *"Treat Me Like a Customer"*. I realized that the journey to that point had been to prepare me for this next season that I would enter.

In some ways I was blinded by the success of the past – the accomplishments achieved – the relationships made – the success earned. But, ultimately, I knew my purpose was to develop leaders to be the best for their families, their organizations, and their communities. It was a scary time that required faith and courage. While I could not see the entire picture, I was brought to the point of choosing faith that my life's journey I had been prepared for this new season through the experiences I had, the relationships I had formed, and the internal strength I had built. It was the best thing I had ever done.

When you come to the edge of all the light you know and are about to step into the darkness of the unknown, faith is knowing that one of two things will happen: There will be something solid to stand on, or you'll be taught to fly.

Elisabeth Kubler-Ross, Swiss American psychiatrist and author

We all face similar situations through life. We all face seasons that require a personal or professional RESET. While some may not be as extreme, all require a point where we stand at a crossroads. Moving forward is scary and requires faith. But, staying where you are will be disastrous to your future.

We're all forced into situations where we need to reevaluate our plans for the future. Often times in life we all face hurdles. We find ourselves on paths we did not expect. We find our selves either getting crushed, or knowing that maybe the path we have chosen, is not heading in the right direction. We can't predict the future. We can't change the past. But we can take comfort in knowing that through each transition in life, greater opportunities exist to live life to the fullest and create the life you imagined.

RESETs come in all shapes and sizes. It could be a dream unrealized. It could be a physical setback, an emotional setback, a financial setback, or a personal setback. These setbacks are part of life. And, although they may tell a story of your past, they don't need to define you as a person. Good, bad, or indifferent, yesterday is behind us. We can't bring it back—but we can create a new version for tomorrow.

A person struggling with a health-issue may never return to find their same physical vitality. But, does that mean they will always be less healthy? No. Why can't they be healthier?

A person struggling through a divorce may never be able to rekindle the flame, but does that mean they will never find love again? No. They may love more.

A person or organization or even a country that struggles through a financial crisis may never be able to return to "the good ole days." But, does that mean they will always struggle financially? No. Our Nation's economy won't ever return to the way it was—it will be different—but does that mean it can't be stronger than before?

As humans, we will face setbacks and changing seasons in life. But, instead of fighting to reclaim the past, we need to learn to fight for the future—because you're still the same definition of you, and your future will not likely be exactly as you planned.

Yes, my past has changed my life in the future. And, so will yours.

RESET!

Acknowledgments

Thanks to the numerous thought leaders and pioneers in the area of personal and professional development who have paved the way through the years and impacted my life in such profound ways.

Thanks to my colleagues who have encouraged, motivated, and "cheered me on" to live my purpose with passion: Louis Upkins, Steve Hayes, Brett Blair, Britt Hunt, Dave Jaworski, Rick Kloete, Jim Fuller, Charles Hagood, Michael Burcham, Dr. Victoria Gamber, Dr. Kelly Chappell, Dr. R. Gordon Williamson, and Dr. Deborah Bushway.

Thanks to all my personal and professional friends—you know who you are—who have been constant cheerleaders and amazing sources of support for me to live my dreams.

Thanks to Suzanne Leonard and Todd Nordstrom for your incredible friendship and guidance in the launch of The RESET Model, book, and brand. Your wisdom and expertise in branding, publishing, and building the platform of thought leaders are amazing, and I am blessed to be part of your growing vision for transforming our world and leaving a legacy.

Special thanks to my bride, Darla, and children, Andrew, Nathanael, and Aleya, for allowing me the opportunity to take time away from our family to pursue my dream of writing and publishing this book. I am blessed to be on this life journey with you.

Finally, I give praise to my Heavenly Father and Lord and Savior, Jesus Christ. I am honored and humbled to be an instrument of Your hand, to bring the message of RESET to the world. I know everyone ends up somewhere but only a very few end up somewhere on purpose. I am excited to be used by You and look forward to even greater opportunities to make an impact in the future – by Your grace and for Your glory.

Beginning Your RESET!

Without continual growth and progress, such words as improvement, achievement, and success have no meaning.
Benjamin Franklin, inventor and visionary

Life balance and clarity of direction are the core aspects that are essential for ultimate success.
Dr. Jason Brooks

Purpose, passion, success: just the sound of these words has an impact on our thoughts, feelings, and attitude. Our hearts beat just a little faster, our attention focuses, and our expectation of experiencing something wonderful is heightened. As we go through life, we often sacrifice much of ourselves and strive to hear these words.

I have observed that the idea of true success is elusive for most. Those who really understand the concept and continue to pursue their success on a daily basis have a special energy and enthusiasm that are immediately evident and clearly different from the vast majority. What I quickly realized has transformed my life. Everyone desires success, but few know how to chart the path to achieve it. This truth was a burden for me, as I thought often about how to help people and companies conceptualize success in a way that is easy to understand, is simple to implement, and addresses the critical point that success is not a destination, but rather a dynamic and continual process that allows for its building over a lifetime.

I have a passion for creating the conditions in which individuals and organizations are able to unleash their greatest potential and achieve their greatest success. This desire has been evident throughout my entire life. Even in childhood, I found joy in seeing others learn, grow, and succeed. I enjoyed seeing my friends in school grasp new concepts as they learned and celebrated with them as they were able to master new knowledge and skills. As I moved into my professional season of life, I have actively pursued roles that allow me to assist in charting the course that helps individuals live their purpose with passion, both personally and professionally, and guide organizations on the journey to success.

But what is success? *Merriam-Webster* defines success as "a degree or measure of succeeding; a favorable or desired outcome; the attainment of wealth, favor, or eminence."[1] Success often is measured by the relative performance or achievement as compared with another.

As we drive down the street, our attention naturally is drawn to the individual who is sitting in the front seat of the newest BMW with leather seats and a moonroof. Our inclination is to evaluate from our paradigm and conclude, "Wow, that person is obviously a great success." We see a husband, wife, and three children enter a restaurant and proceed to share a meal, with all members talking openly, laughing, and enjoying the time together. As we watch from the table nearby, we think, "Gosh, what a happy family. They have it all together and are really successful."

In reality, however, we simply do not know the hearts of others. Success, as measured in comparison to the societal norm or the accomplishments of others, is fleeting. In the end, the greatest measure of success—your success—is how you are living each and every minute in alignment with your purpose.

Living in alignment with your purpose, however, sometimes means that change is needed. Often we are living our lives more as observers and passive participants, rather than as confident, courageous, disciplined authors of our destiny. To get on track and to realign with our purpose, many of us come to a point where we need to RESET. We need to push the button to evaluate who we are and the choices we are making and deliberately decide that a change is needed in order to live our true purpose and achieve the greatest measure of success.

Just as Louis Upkins was forced to confront times of RESET in his life in which the expectations he had for himself and his future were changed, so too will each of us face similar seasons. During these times, we have choices to make. We can allow our feelings of loss and unmet expectations to consume us or we can RESET by viewing our life through the new lens of opportunity and hope for an amazing future.

I have met with individuals considered by worldly standards to be among the most successful people in the world. But in speaking with them, I find that they are utterly broken and miserable. They find no joy in their accomplishments and view all of their striving as being in vain and at the whim of others. By contrast, I have met those who would seem to be lacking from a societal measure of success but are full of joy, happiness, and contentment and living a life of purpose with passion.

There are successful people everywhere, but they are not necessarily easy to find. When you have the pleasure of encountering these individuals, however, you recognize their success immediately. There is lightness in their demeanor. There is a spirit of expectancy that permeates all that they do. There is a sense of hopefulness for the future as they strive each and every day to live the purpose that was created in them. These are the people who truly are successful.

I believe that everyone, in one way or another, needs a RESET. I believe that everyone wants to be successful. Everyone wants to experience the freedom that comes from knowing and living out their purpose, which in the end leads to true success. I believe that a RESET that ultimately results in success is available and can be achieved by everyone, including you who are reading this book. You can live your purpose and experience the full success you were destined to achieve!

RESET, however, is not the same for everyone. Some may need a "Radical RESET" that will require making a sharp turn from the direction they are currently taking. You know when your life is headed in the wrong direction and a drastic change is required. When I think of those in need of a Radical RESET, my mind goes to the adolescents who I worked with during my clinical internship and residency at Skyline Madison. These teens were admitted to our inpatient behavior health unit with significant issues, such as alcohol and drug addiction, unhealthy sexual behavior, family crisis situations, oppositional defiant behavior issues, eating disorders, and other self-harming behaviors, to name just a few. For some, true mental illness was the issue. Others made choices that took them down a road that would have led to continued pain and ultimate destruction of themselves and their lives. These teens, in one way or another, were in need of a Radical RESET to help them completely turn from the path they were on and create a healthy life. These RESETS are not easy, but they are essential!

Others may need a "Realigning RESET." In general, their life is on track. They are living a life of relative success, making a difference in their relationships and work and giving to others through their time, talent, and treasure. They are satisfied and generally happy but know that there is something that could be better—something that is just a little off. Most of us would fall into this category. We are satisfied, yet we know we can do more, live more, love more, give more, and be more.

The final reset is a "Refining RESET." This is for those who are living their dreams and living their purpose with passion. There is clarity of self and an understanding of how their life impacts the lives of others in a positive way. The Refining RESET is a continual process that helps to ensure that they stay on track and in alignment with their purpose day by day, week by week, month by month, and year by year. In reality, staying focused on a vivid image of our purpose is essential to remaining on course. It is the daily discipline of refining that results in living the life we have always dreamed of living.

The RESET we pursue is not a destination, but rather a lifelong journey. In addition, it is important to remember that any structure that we desire to sustain over time must be built on a strong and stable foundation. In this case, that foundation is established through the concepts of balance and direction as presented by The RESET Model. While there may be other approaches to achieving a degree of success, I have found that building a life based on strong models and principles allow for the ability to stay on course and committed to results. I believe The RESET Model is a structure or framework to help you conceptualize and begin your own journey to reformatting your purpose to live the life you always imagined. There is nothing magical or mystical about this approach, but I believe that by integrating these ideas into your journey, you will be able to live your purpose with passion.

While the concepts in this book are relatively simple to understand, the path to living them daily is not. It will require discipline and a deep commitment to restoring your wellness in the seven aspects of life balance that include emotional, social, spiritual, physical, intellectual, occupational and financial. You will need to reformat and redefine your life purpose, renew your passion, recreate your plan to achieve your success, recognize obstacles to living your life of purpose, and refocus on giving thanks for all you have been given, which ultimately involves celebrating the fullness of your success. Through our journey together you will:

- RESET Your Relationships—Do you have positive relationships with your family and a close group of friends you enjoy spending time with? Are you lifted up by your relationships, or do they often seem to weigh you down? You will evaluate the relationships in your life and make decisions regarding where changes would be important.

- RESET Your Spirituality—Do you have a great sense of self and your impact on this world? Do you have an understanding of a world greater than your own? You will explore this essential area of life and establish daily disciplines to grow to even deeper levels of spiritual awareness and enlightenment.

- RESET Your Health—Do you have areas of your life in which your physical wellness could be improved? You will identify those areas that could be better and establish goals to live a healthier life.

- RESET Your Career—Do you enjoy your job and career path? Do you experience a sense of fulfillment in your chosen profession by using your knowledge, skills, talents, and abilities to make a difference? You will assess your career satisfaction and create a path to even greater fulfillment in your work.

- RESET Your Finances—Are you satisfied with your financial situation? Does your money run out before the month does? You will evaluate your current finances and develop a plan to achieve all of your financial goals and dreams.

- RESET Your Learning—How are you investing in yourself? You will begin to focus on self-development and create a plan to grow as an individual.

- RESET Your Purpose—Why are you here? What were you created to achieve? You will embark on a journey to understand the essence of you and crystallize your mission, vision, values, and picture of success.

- RESET Your Passion—Why do you do what you do? What is your innate motivation? You will answer this question and identify the driving forces in your life that push you to live your purpose.

- RESET Your Plans—Do you have a process for creating

your life plans and holding yourself accountable for accomplishing those plans? You will learn about the process of goal development and the steps for ensuring you achieve those goals.

- RESET Your Life!

Your RESET, and ultimately success in your life, likely will not come easy, but I assure you that once you begin the journey, you will never look back.Each of us is on a unique journey in life. We have the chance to pursue our own purpose, our own passion, and our own plans and live a life that is uniquely our own. Excitement comes when our individual paths connect in such a way that we can share in the experiences of others while pursuing our own purpose and ultimate success. Louis Upkins experienced incredible success in his early professional career as a marking and branding guru. However, he always knew that he had a desire to marry and build a family. While he was living a life of great "success", he knew that lifestyle was not in alignment with his ultimately goals and dreams. He needed a RESET.

The man Louis is today is the product of his passion for his family, family, friends, and clients. He realized early on that a successful life is created and lived when we understand that we are dynamic and all aspects of life are interconnected. He created a clear picture in his mind of what the future would be and began the process of living that future. Through the years, Louis has touched the lives of many and left a legacy of success and significance for all he has encountered.

My heart's desire is to take the gifts that have been entrusted to me and use them to communicate a strategy to help you achieve the greatest success possible—one that is in alignment with your innate purpose.

My prayer is that in the pages to follow, you will grow in three areas. First, I hope that you will develop a great understanding of the foundational laws that govern our life experiences. Next, I hope that you will gain awareness of your personal balance and establish plans and commit to change that will allow you to experience an even greater sense of balance in your life or in the life of your organization. And finally, I hope that you will achieve clarity of your purpose and passion, enabling you to chart the path forward toward unleashing your full potential and achieving success.

Through this work, I will introduce you to ideas, concepts, and a proven model to RESET your life as you begin your journey toward success. My hope and dream is that you embrace wholeheartedly this model and achieve increased awareness of self, the establishment of a clear direction, and the success that you have dreamed of all your life.

I have devoted much of my life to working with individuals and organizations to help them achieve greater levels of success. In my research and work, I have found that many of us live lives that are out of balance. Ultimately, imbalance leads to significant distress and keeps us from being able to be as successful as possible. I have also found that the vast majority of people go through the motions of life in much the same manner as a boat on the ocean being tossed back and forth by the waves; they are often unaware of the final destination or how to create the conditions to arrive there. Through my work, I have seen many people gain greater clarity of purpose, experience increased life balance and overall wellness, and start on the path toward achieving their life dreams, goals, and success through the use of the concepts that I will present to you.

As you read this, ask yourself the tough questions, but also create an environment in which you can make choices that will release you from living a life of mediocrity so that you can live one of extravagant balance, purpose, passion, and success.

The time to begin is now. Your RESET is waiting for you!

The RESET Model

As a launching point for our time together, it is important to discuss the foundational concepts that form the basis of the journey to RESET. The idea of RESET came to me almost three years ago.

My heart always has been deeply burdened by my desire to be a catalyst leader for those who are seeking greater purpose and a reset in their lives. While driving home pondering these ideas one day, I saw a vivid picture in my mind. Suddenly I understood two essential elements that were critical for living a life of purpose, passion, and success. Scrambling to find a pen and scrap piece of paper in the car as I drove along the interstate, I was overcome with emotion and excitement over the picture that was elevated to my conscious mind. I had done considerable work in the area of life balance through my doctoral dissertation and knew through my research that this was a critical aspect for success. In addition, through my experiences of working in the areas of personal and organizational strategic planning, I understood the importance of purpose and creating a plan to achieve that purpose. Not until that moment, however, had the two converged into what is now The RESET Model, a real-world blueprint for dynamically linking together these two concepts and for recognizing that to achieve true success, a RESET is often needed—a RESET of our balance and of our direction.

I remember feeling exhilarated as I arrived home. I shared with my wife this revelation that had eluded me for years. Her excitement joined my own as together we realized that I had broken through layers of theory and observation into a new dimension of understanding and that this was a topic that would have great interest to many individuals who were struggling with creating the conditions for unleashing their full purpose and potential in their lives.

The RESET Model is the lens through which you will begin to clearly see your quest. Note that there are three essential elements in the model that work dynamically and harmoniously together to allow you to achieve your own and unique experience of success.

The RESET Model is based on three core concepts. The first is the understanding of certain foundational laws that operate and impact our ability to realize the greatest degree of success possible. These laws are not unique to my work, but I have found that they are highly relevant and create the conditions for success for individuals and organizations. The Law of the Harvest, the Law of Diminishing Intent, the Law of Reciprocity, and the Law of Attraction are constantly in action, and the choices you make either amplify or minimize the impact of these laws. Just as we are subject to the laws of physics, so too are we subject to these laws that form the foundation of our life experience.

The second is the concept of life balance. I devoted my doctoral dissertation research to understanding the impact of life balance on corporate executives. My research and the work of others reveal that each aspect of life affects the others. Just as a gyroscope is used to maintain stability by airplane pilots, so too does life balance create stability in our lives. While it may be nice to say that physical wellness is not related to the ability to be successful and fulfilled in one's job (occupational wellness), that simply is not the case. In order to create the conditions for the greatest success, we each need to strive daily for the greatest sense of balance possible. The aspects of physical, social, emotional, spiritual, occupational, intellectual, and financial wellness will be explored in great detail in the section on "Life Balance," and you will have an opportunity to evaluate your own sense of balance and then develop action plans that can result in achieving a greater sense of balance.

The third dimension of The RESET Model is that of direction. We can have the greatest sense of balance possible, but if we do not have a clear understanding of who we are or where we are going, success will elude us. Much like a compass that is used to provide the bearings and coordinates for our destination, the P^{4}G Model, a sub-model of The RESET Model, provides the framework from which to understand our purpose, unleash our passion, create plans and goals to achieve our purpose, overcome obstacles that seek to stand in our way, and celebrate the achievement of our success. The P^{4}G Model will be presented and explored in detail in the section on "Direction." You will take time to evaluate your life, create a vision of success for yourself, establish the plans necessary to achieve that vision, and appreciate how, by continually moving through the process while keeping a focus on maintaining the greatest sense of balance, you will live your life of success.

The RESET Model brings these three areas together in a concise structure that will allow you to evaluate your current situation and create a path for living your purpose with passion. While all areas are no doubt connected, it is also easy to break each apart and establish plans and behaviors around them separately. It is through the dynamic nature of this process that you will be able to chart the course for your life, begin your RESET, and continue the journey indefinitely.

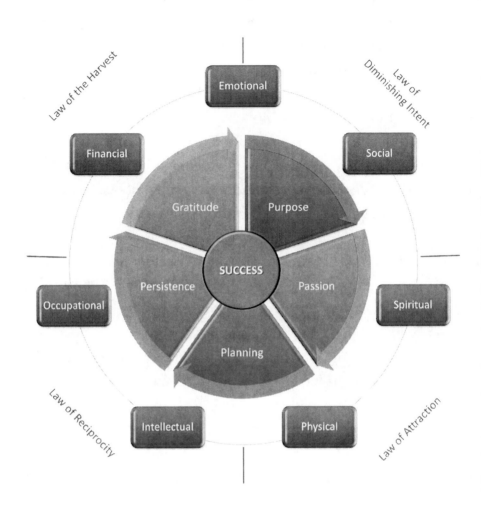

The RESET Model

Begin at the End

The journey of a thousand miles begins with a single step
Lao-Tzu, Chinese philosopher

At the heart of RESET is the idea that we all must begin at the end. One universal truth is that at some point in time, we will all face the end of our lives. Unless our end comes suddenly and through tragic events, as we near the end we will have the opportunity to reflect on our years and the impact our lives made. What will your life story say? What will be the legacy of your years?

Through this book, you will be led on a personal journey to explore multiple areas of your life and create the life you were destined to live. Before beginning any journey, it is important to know where you are today and where you are going. With the concept of starting with the end firmly in mind, we will begin by engaging in a powerful visualization and writing experience to help you think through those very questions and visualize the picture of your life and the purpose you were destined to live.

First, find several blank pieces of paper. On the top of the first page, write, "The Life of…" and your name. Next, create in your mind's eye a vivid picture as you slowly read the following:

Imagine for a moment that you are standing in front of an audience, looking out into the crowd at many faces. Their expressions are sad, sorrowful, and sympathetic.

You realize quickly by scanning the room that you are giving a eulogy at a funeral. To your surprise, this funeral happens to be your own.

What will you say about your own life? Your work? Your relationships?

Your legacy?

What is the expression on your face? Are you sad and full of a sense of loss and regret, not because you've passed, but because you didn't live the life you imagined?

Let's take some time together to begin the process of creating a picture of the life that you imagined. Regardless of the stage you are currently at in life, you have a story to tell. You have the story of the past, the story of the present, and the story of the future.

As you begin the process of writing your story, use the following as a guide to lead your thoughts and writing. There are some points to remember as you begin this journey, however. First, you should complete this over the course of several days or even weeks, taking time to really search your memory of the past and your heart for the dreams of your future. Do not rush through the process, as the experience is in many ways even more important than the written results. As you go through the experience, you may have thoughts and emotions that surface that you have not experienced in a long time. Some may be happy and joyful, while others may be sorrowful and painful. Identify someone you can talk to about the experience. If there are painful memories from your past that surface, you may need to contact a counselor or helping professional to process and work through some of the feelings. Remember that you are not alone and that this is part of your growth and journey process. While we are in some ways a product of our past, we are not held captive by it. You are not only reflecting on the past, but are also scripting the story for your future. That is what "begin at the end" is all about. Through this experience, you are writing the story of your future and what you dream your future will be.

The Early Years

Think about the time from your earliest memories to age eleven. As you reflect on this time, answer the following questions:

1. Where were you born?

2. Who were your parents? What were their names?

3. Did you have any brothers or sisters? What were their names?

4. Where did you live during your early childhood years?

5. What were your first memories?

6. Where did you go to elementary school?

7. Who were your closest friends during this time?

8. Who were your favorite teachers?

9. What did you like to do as a child?

10. What are your most vivid memories of your childhood?

11. What emotions come to you when you think of your childhood? What makes you happy when thinking about this time? What makes you sad? What brings you fear? What brings you comfort?

The Adolescent Years

Think about the time from age twelve to age eighteen. As you reflect on this time, answer the following questions:

1. Where did you live during this time?

2. Who lived with you?

3. What do you remember of your parents during this time? What was your relationship like with them?

4. What do you remember of your brothers and sisters during this time? What was your relationship like with them?

5. Where did you go to middle school? Where did you go to high school?

6. Who were your closest friends during this time?

7. What did you like to do as a teen? What were your hobbies? What were the extracurricular activities you were involved with in school?

8. What were your favorite subjects in school?

9. Who were your favorite teachers?

10. Where was your first job? What was that like?

11. What are your most vivid memories of your adolescent years?

12. What were your greatest successes during this time?

13. What challenges did you face during this time?

14. Who did you have romantic relationships with? What were these relationships like?

15. What emotions come to you when you think of your teenage years? What makes you happy when you think about this time? What makes you sad? What brings you fear? What brings you comfort?

16. Think about your spiritual journey during this time. Did you have an understanding of spiritual things? Where did that understanding come from? How did it develop for you?

17. What was your physical health like during this time?

Late Adolescence and Early Adulthood

1. Think about the time from age eighteen to age thirty. As you reflect on this time, answer the following questions:

2. Where did you live during this time?

3. Who lived with you?

4. What do you remember about your parents during this time? What was yourrelationship like with them?

5. What do you remember of your brothers and sisters during this time? What was your relationship like with them?

6. Where did you work during this time?

7. Did you go to college? If so, where?

8. What was it like going to college?

9. Who were your closest friends?

10. What are some memories you have about your friends?

11. What was your field of study?

12. What were your favorite subjects?

13. Who were your favorite teachers?

14. What were your greatest successes during this time?

15. What challenges did you face during this time?

16. Who did you have romantic relationships with? What were these relationships like?

17. What emotions come to you when you think of your late adolescent and earlyadult years? What makes you happy when you think about this time? What makes you sad? What brings you fear? What brings you comfort?

18. Think about your spiritual journey during this time. Did you have an understanding of spiritual things? Where did that understanding come from? How did it develop for you?

19. What was your physical health like during this time?

Adulthood

Think about the time from age thirty to age sixty . As you reflect on this time, answer the following questions:

1. Where did you live during this time?

2. Who lived with you?

3. Who did you have romantic relationships with? What were these relationships like?

4. When did you get married (if applicable)?

5. Whom did you marry? Where did you meet?

6. What is the relationship like with your spouse?

7. What do you like to do together as a couple?

8. Do you have children? If so, how many? Are they boys or girls? What are their names?

9. What are the relationships like in your family?

10. Write about your family vacations and times spent together. What do you like to do together as a family?

11. What strengths do you have as a family?

12. What challenges do you have as a family?

13. What are some memories you have about your family?

14. What do you remember about your parents during this time? What was your relationship like with them?

15. What do you remember of your brothers and sisters during this time?

16. What was relationship like with them?

17. Write about your career journey during your adult years. Where did you work during this time? What jobs did you hold?

18. What were your greatest career successes?

19. What were your greatest career challenges?

20. What did you enjoy most about your career?

21. What was most frustrating for you about your work?

22. Who were your closest friends?

23. What are some memories you have about your friends?

24. What were your greatest successes during this time?

25. What challenges did you face during this time?

26. What emotions come to you when you think of your adult years? What makes you happy when you think about this time? What makes you sad? What brings you fear? What brings you comfort?

27. Think about your spiritual journey during this time. Did you have an understanding of spiritual things? Where did that understanding come from? How did it develop for you?

28. What was your physical health like during this time?

29. What was your financial situation like during this time?

Late Adulthood

Think about the time from age sixty and beyond. As you reflect on this time, answer the following questions:

1. Where did you live during this time?

2. Were you married or in a committed relationship? If so, with whom?

3. What is the relationship like with your spouse?

4. What do you like to do together as a couple?

5. What are the relationships like in your family?

6. Write about your family vacations and times spent together. What do
you like to do together as a family?

7. What is your relationship like with your children?

8. Do you have grandchildren? What is your relationship like with your grandchildren?

9. What strengths do you have as a family?

10. What challenges do you have as a family?

11. What are some memories you have about your family?

12. What do you remember about your parents during this time? What was your relationship like with them?

13. When did your parents pass away? What was that like for you?

14. What do you remember of your brothers and sisters during this time?

15. What was relationship like with them?

16. Write about your career journey during your late adult years. Where did you work during this time (if applicable)? What jobs did you hold?

17. What were your greatest career successes?

18. What were your greatest career challenges?

19. What did you enjoy most about your career?

20. What was most frustrating for you about your work?

21. Who were your closest friends?

22. What are some memories you have about your friends?

23. What were your greatest successes during this time?

24. What challenges did you face during this time?

25. What emotions come to you when you think of your late adulthood years? What makes you happy when you think about this time? What makes you sad? What brings you fear? What brings you comfort?

26. Think about your spiritual journey during this time. Did you have an understanding of spiritual things? Where did that understanding come from? How did it develop for you?

27. What was your physical health like during this time?

28. What was your financial situation like during this time?

Your Passing

1. Think about the time of your passing. As you reflect on this time, answer the following questions:

2. How old were you when you passed away?

3. Where did you live in the final years of your life?

4. Who survived your passing (spouse, children, grandchildren)?

5. Who were your closest friends?

6. What were the greatest accomplishments of your life?

7. What were the greatest challenges you faced in your life?

8. How did you give back to others?

9. What did you stand for? What was the essence of your character?

10. As you think of statements that others would share about you at your funeral, what would they write?
    a. Your spouse?

    b. Your children?

    c. Your grandchildren?

    d. Your coworkers?

    e. Your friends?

f. Your spiritual leader?

g. Your physician?

h. Your teachers?

i. Yourself? What would you say about yourself?

j. As you look back over the story of your life, come up with one statement that encapsulates the life you lived and the legacy you leave behind.

There is no doubt that completing this exercise will give you a powerful opportunity to reflect on the past and visualize your future. It will help to paint a clear picture of what you truly desire your life to mean and the difference that you are seeking to make. As we continue on our journey through RESET, you will come back to these writings as you evaluate your life today, compare it to the life you desire for yourself, and establish plans to live that life. Ultimately, at the end of our lives, we will be able to reflect on how we lived our lives in alignment with our purpose.

Foundational Laws of Success

Whatever the human mind can conceive and believe it can also achieve.
Napoleon Hill, author of "Think and Grow Rich"

The basis of any resilient and sustained structure is achieved first by establishing a strong foundation. According to Merriam-Webster, a foundation is an "underlying base or support upon which something is built. It can also be a principle or principles that create the basis upon which other concepts are placed."[1] Through the ages, philosophers, scientists, and leading thinkers have sought to explore and understand general and fundamental concepts related to:

- Metaphysics (nature of reality)
- Epistemology (nature and scope of knowledge)
- Ethics (morality)
- Politics (relationship between individuals)
- Aesthetics (beauty and perception)
- Logic (valid argument forms)
- Religion (sense of connection to higher power)

As theories and ideas have emerged in these areas, they have led to the creation of foundational principles that provide the basis upon which human experience and life can be understood and built.

Four laws provide a foundation upon which success can be built and realized. Although these laws may not always be in our conscious awareness, they are nonetheless constantly at work in our lives, moving us closer to or further away from our success.

It is important to understand these laws and realize that while they cannot be changed, we are able to modify our behavior in response to these laws, giving us the ability to maximize our potential to achieving our greatest success.

Foundational Laws of Success

The Law of the Harvest

The law of the harvest is to reap more than you sow. Sow and act, and you
reap a habit. Sow a habit and you reap a character.
Sow a character and you reap a destiny.
James Allen, philosopher and author

The first of the four foundational laws of success is based on the natural occurrence of sowing and reaping. You begin to realize that in the natural course of life, you ultimately will reap that which you sow. If you sow discontent, anxiety, doubt, and fear, you will reap the same. However, if you sow self-contentment, security, clarity, and confidence, that will be your experience.

Stephen R. Covey, author of the highly acclaimed *The 7 Habits of Highly Effective People*, states:

> Did you ever consider how ridiculous it would be to try to cram on a farm—to forget to plant in the spring, play all summer, and then cram in the fall to bring in the harvest? The farm is a natural system. The price must be paid, and the process followed. You always reap what you sow; there is no shortcut.[2]

It is important to remember that inherent in the Law of the Harvest is the physical reality that we all pass through different seasons of life. Just as the farmer is bound to the cycle of nature and the seasons, so too must we experience those seasons in our own lives. Each of these seasons holds special purpose, which ultimately leads to the fulfillment of the Law of the Harvest.

Spring is the time of planting. It is the time of newness, rebirth, and anticipation for dreaming of results in the future. Often during the springtime of our lives, we experience increased creativity and passion for seeing things through a fresh lens. We see the potential and opportunity in the future and are excited to begin planting the seeds for success for that future.

Summer is the time of tending and nurturing. Focus turns from planting to caring for the growing plants. This time requires constant effort and focus to ensure that the seedlings of success that were planted receive the needed sunshine, rain, and nutrients and that the weeds that would seek to choke out the plants of the harvest are immediately removed from the field. For many this is the time of greatest effort. We must continually nurture and tend to the needs of the crops that are growing. Likewise, we must be aware of the weeds and other circumstances that would seek to choke out or destroy the harvest. It is not a time for relaxation but rather for consistent, persistent, diligent effort and commitment, looking forward to the next season when the fruit of the labor is realized.

Fall is the time of harvest. It is during this time that we reap what we have sown and nurtured. We often feel great excitement and a sense of accomplishment as we collect the harvest and can celebrate the successes of our efforts. While there is certainly effort to be invested in the harvest, taking time to experience a sense of gratitude is essential. There are some seasons when the harvest is abundant and others when it is lacking. Ultimately, however, we each need to take an opportunity to give thanks for all we are given and for the ability to reap what has been sown, nurtured, and protected.

Winter is the time of dreaming, reflecting, and planning for the coming spring. Although winter brings to mind thoughts of cold, dreary days and long nights, winter ultimately is a time of reflection, preparation, and anticipation. It is when we can look forward to "what will be." It is a time to think back on the previous season and answer the following questions: What went well? What did not go well? What could have been done differently? While it is essential that we do not become a prisoner to the past, it is important to take opportunities to learn from the past so we can make decisions for a more successful, passionate, and purposeful future. Winter also is a time to look forward to the coming spring and make plans for the next season of planting, tending, and harvest.

What is my goal? What is my plan? What will I plant? Where will I plant? How will I plant? What resources will I need to be successful? All of these questions should be considered during the season of winter so that when spring arrives, you will have a clear focus as the cycle begins again.

While the Law of the Harvest and experience of the season are universal, unanticipated situations can arise and have a catastrophic impact on the harvest. One example occurred in 2010, when a quarter of the Russian wheat crops were lost due to an unexpected drought and record heat wave that ravaged the region.[3] This certainly was unanticipated by the Russian people and had a catastrophic impact on the Russian economy, sending prices for wheat soaring around the world. During such times in our lives, we tend to cower under the weight of perceived defeat and to project that defeat into all areas of life. However, we must remember that such events are part of the cycle and mystery of life and often are impossible to anticipate. In these times, hope arises by remembering that rarely do devastating losses occur year after year and season after season. Rather, with the coming of a new spring, summer, fall, and winter, the ability to again plant, tend, harvest, and plan is presented anew. Success can be achieved again.

As you consider your own life, you must constantly evaluate yourself in relationship to this foundational law. Take time now to answer these questions about yourself regarding the Law of the Harvest.

1. What season are you currently in (spring, summer, fall, or winter) in your personal life? How about your professional life? Your volunteer life? Other areas of life?

2. What are you dreaming about accomplishing in the next season of your life?

3. What are you doing to take advantage of all this season has to offer?

4. What are you doing today to prepare for the next season?

5. How have you seen the Law of the Harvest in action in your own life in the past?

The Law of Diminishing Intent

The longer you wait to do something you know you should do now,
the greater the chances you will never actually do it.
Bob Burg, Author of "The Go-Giver"

The Law of Diminishing Intent was discussed in detail by the late Jim Rohn, who was regarded as one of the most influential motivational speakers and authors of this generation on the topics of self-development, performance, and success. As a fervent student of leadership and personal growth principles, Rohn recognized that a significant difference between those who realize success and those who do not is the ability and desire to immediately act. From this observation came the Law of Diminishing Intent, which suggests that the longer you wait to do something that you know you should do, the greater the chance it will never actually be done. As you consider the events that you would characterize as missed opportunities in your life, did the Law of Diminishing Intent come into play? Whenever we rationalize that we should not act when opportunities come and go, we become desensitized over time to the emotional fuel that is released through new adventures to expand, grow, and realize our full potential. This cycle, if allowed to continue, eventually leads to paralysis of spirit.

A driving force to action is emotion. When emotion is high, motivation also is high. Recall an experience in your life when you desired to act but did not. Maybe it was that special someone in high school who you wanted desperately to ask out on a date. Your heart was pounding, your hands were sweating, and your knees were weak as you approached your heartthrob in the hallway. Although you had rehearsed the right words to say for weeks, the moment of action made you suddenly feel like your feet were planted in cinder blocks and every step required all your strength. As you approached this moment of truth, at just the last second, you stepped to the other side of the hallway and continued walking, deciding instead to honor the fear of potential failure by avoiding that special someone. From that point forward, the desire continued to diminish until eventually the motivation to speak up was completely gone. Most of us have faced such a situation and wonder years later, "What kept me from taking the risk?" or "Why didn't I just talk to them?" Although not necessarily filled with regret, we often ponder what might have been and how we may have been different if only we had decided to act at the moment of inspiration.

We must learn to maximize the value of emotion in being a catalyst for action and change by minimizing the natural tendency to evaluate, rationalize, and resist change. Newton's First Law of Motion, sometimes referred to as the Law of Inertia, states that objects at rest tend to stay at rest and objects in motion tend to stay in motion. This law, although initially presented to explain objects in the physical world, also applies to behavior and action of individuals. We are predisposed to find a point of "comfort" (an arbitrary concept defined by each individual) and most often are content to remain in that place or state. At the same time, we are continually growing and becoming. We were created for greatness and with a purpose—one that continues through our lives. As a result, we constantly battle between realizing our greatest potential and surrendering to the tendency to remain where we are. Over time, emotion and passion— the catalysts for change—are replaced with logic and reason, which naturally encourage us to stay where we are and avoid the risks associated with change. In the end, however, every action or inaction is accompanied by inherent risk. By embracing the impact of the Law of Diminishing Intent, we can make the choice to take the risk of change, realizing that some outcomes will be positive, and others not. Ultimately, we are growing and moving along the path toward realizing our greatest success.

As you consider your own life, you must constantly evaluate yourself in relation to this foundational law. Take time now to answer these questions about yourself regarding The Law of Diminishing Intent:

1. What should you do right now that you have resisted doing in the past?

2. What is holding you back from acting today?

3. What emotions do you feel when you think about the action you should be taking today to realize success in the future?

4. How have you seen the Law of Diminishing Intent in action in your own life in the past?

The Law of Attraction

"For as he thinks in his heart, so is he"
Proverbs 23:7, Holy Bible

The third of the foundational laws of success is the Law of Attraction. Essentially, the Law of Attraction states that we attract to ourselves that which we give our focus, attention, and energy to. It is important to understand that this law applies to both those things that are wanted and unwanted. This law's counterpart in the physical world is the elemental law of physics establishing that "like attracts like." James Allen stated "the soul attracts that which it secretly harbors, that which it loves, and also that which it fears; it reaches the height of its cherished aspirations; it falls to the level of its unchastened desires, and circumstances are the means by which the soul receives its own."[4]

According to Jack Canfield, best-selling author, speaker, and coach, "Simply put, the Law of Attraction states that you will attract into your life whatever you focus on. Whatever you give your energy and attention to will come back to you. So, if you stay focused on the good and positive things in your life, you will automatically attract more good and positive things into your life."[5] It is important to understand that we attract that which we place our focus on, whether positive or negative.

Rhonda Byrne, author of *The Secret,* quoted Lisa Nichols, an author and personal empowerment advocate, who stated that the Law of Attraction is constantly at work:

> Any time your thoughts are flowing, the law of attraction is working. When you're thinking about the past, the law of attraction's working. When you're thinking about the present or the future, the law of attraction is working. It's an ongoing process. You don't press pause, you don't press stop. It is forever in action, as your thoughts are.[6]

As humans, we have the unique ability to choose where we place our thoughts. We have the choice to meditate and focus on the positive, uplifting, and inspirational. We also have the choice to think about things that are self-defeating, self-limiting, and demotivational. In the end, when we focus on those things that are in harmony with success, we are more likely to realize that success.

While the Law of Attraction is not new and is prevalent in the thoughts of many cultures and societies, it is important to understand that this law is not a "name it and claim it" philosophy. It is not enough to think "I am..." or "I have..." The Law of Attraction creates the conduit by which inspiration and motivation can grow. Ultimately, however, thought without action is fruitless. The Law of Attraction is one of the four foundational laws that are essential for the building of a life of balance, focus, and success. But it is this law in combination with action that brings to life the reality of that success.

There is universal understanding that through the Law of Attraction, the subconscious is able to create the path to realizing our dreams. While we do not fully understand the ways and means by which our conscious mind connects with our subconscious to bring to life the desires of our heart, it is clear that our lack of understanding does not negate the reality of the existence of this law. Earl Nightingale stated, "Throughout all history, the great wise men and teachers, philosophers, and prophets have all disagreed with one another on many different things. It is only on this one point that they are in complete and unanimous agreement."[7]

Embrace this foundational law of success to experience a transformation of thought into reality that will truly astound you.

As you consider your own life, you must constantly evaluate yourself in relationship to this foundational law. Take time now to answer these questions about yourself regarding The Law of Attraction.

1. What do most of your thoughts focus on?

2. Where are you placing the majority of your mental energy? Your physical energy? Your emotional energy?

3. What positive thoughts are you focusing on that will help you to realize your success?

4. What negative thoughts are you allowing to creep into your mind?

5. How have you seen the Law of Attraction in action in your life in the past?

57

The Law of Reciprocity

Therefore, whatever you want men to do to you, do also to them.
Matthew 7:12, Holy Bible

The fourth and final of the foundational laws of success is the Law of Reciprocity. The Law of Reciprocity states that we give and take mutually. In other words, in the natural course of life, we will have returned to us in the same manner in which we give. Think to a time when someone gave something to you. When you did receive from someone else, what was your natural response? When others give to us, there is a natural tendency for us to want to give back. Similarly, when we give to others, there is a sense of obligation from them to give back to us. This law is about giving and receiving. That which you give you shall also receive.

The Law of Reciprocity is closely related to the Law of the Harvest in that what we reap depends on the kind of seed that we plant. What a man sows is followed by the foundational law of "kind reproduces kind." Consider, for example, that you planted a pear tree in your backyard. Would you expect to find oranges on that tree when it comes time for harvest? Of course not! That would be crazy, and you do not have to worry about that. You can rest assured that you absolutely will find pears on you pear tree. This concept is illustrated by a parable shared by Jesus in Luke 6:43–45, which states, "For a good tree does not bear bad fruit, nor does a bad tree bear good fruit. For every tree is known by its fruit. For men do not gather figs from thorns, nor do they gather grapes from a bramble bush. A good man out of the good treasure of his heart brings forth good; and an evil man out of the evil treasure of his heart brings forth evil. For out of the abundance of the heart his mouth speaks."

To realize the full potential of the Law of Reciprocity, all parties must benefit from the relationship and invest in the relationship. Actions must be mutually rewarding or an imbalance in reciprocity is created. When it comes to success in your life, the Law of Reciprocity will help you gain the success in unparalleled returns. The more you help others gain what they are looking for, the more you will be helped. It may not seem like this is the case on the surface, but you cannot give without receiving.

The Law of Reciprocity often is a challenge for us to embrace. We understand the law and celebrate when we see it manifest in others' lives. However, there is a tendency to become frustrated or discouraged if the reciprocity does not occur in the way or timing that we expect or anticipate.

Just as the harvest does not necessarily occur at the same time every season, the returns from our investment in others will not necessarily be the same from situation to situation. We have often heard the Golden Rule that states, "Do unto others as you would have them do unto you." While this is certainly a noble intent, this approach is foundationally self-focused, as it suggests that that you are acting through the lens of what would be best for you. I would encourage a different course that states: "Do unto others as they would have you do unto them." Through this paradigm, you truly are living an empathic mindset by placing yourself in the position of other individuals, seeking to understand their perspectives, needs, and desires, and acting in a way to help them achieve all they desire. From that, others necessarily will act in kind by "doing unto you as you would have done unto you." While this is a slight variation on a concept that is prevalent through many world cultures and religions, it would seem to be in alignment with providing an essential foundation for valuing each individual, investing in others, and building ultimate success.

We each have the ability to give of ourselves to positively impact the lives of others. Although it's a little gesture, I love the mornings when I am waiting in the line at Starbucks for my "daily inspiration" and am surprised when I arrived at the window to hear, "The person in front of you already covered it." There is something about that experience that makes me want to "pay it forward" and do the same for the guest behind me. It is at those moments that I just know it is going to be a great day!

As you consider your own life, you must constantly evaluate yourself in relationship to this foundational law. Take time now to answer these questions about yourself regarding the Law of Reciprocity.

1. What are you doing today to invest in the success of others?

2. What are you doing today to give to others?

3. How are you helping others achieve their hopes and dreams?

4. How have you seen the Law of Reciprocity in action in your life in the past?

Final Thoughts

The foundational laws of success work in harmony to create a foundation through which life balance, direction, and ultimately success can be realized.

As you take time to continually evaluate where you are in relation to these laws, you will realize the ability to use the strength of these concepts in your life. Learn how to apply the principles of the Law of the Harvest, the Law of Diminishing Intent, the Law of

Attraction, and the Law of Reciprocity to create an environment that affords you the ability to realize your full potential and success. Each individual's path to success is continual and unique. However, these laws, which are universal, when understood and applied to your life, provide the foundation upon which your purpose, passion, goals, and successful RESET will be achieved.

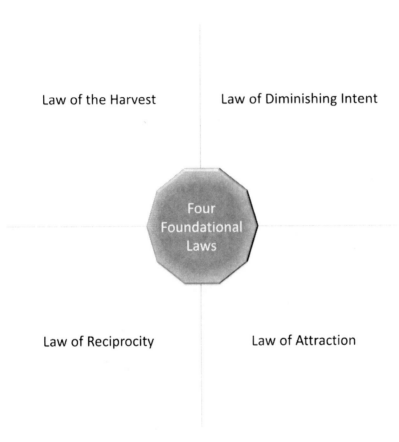

Foundational Laws of Success

The Aspects of Life Balance

We can be sure that the greatest hope for maintaining equilibrium in the face of any situation rests within ourselves.
Francis J. Braceland, former chief psychiatrist of the Institute of Living

We have overstretched our personal boundaries and forgotten that true success comes from living an authentic life fueled with a sense of purpose and balance.
Dr. Kathleen Hall, founder and CEO of The Stress Institute and Mindful Living Network

We were created for balance. Just think about the mutual equilibrium of our bodies. We have two eyes, two ears, two arms, two hands, two legs, and two feet. Even the physical features we have only one of are symmetrically positioned on our bodies. This was not by accident. Our bodily balance provides stability and functionally that allows us to walk, carry objects, and see and hear to discern precise locations. Just like our bodies, our lives require balance in order to be effective.

To characterize the importance of balance in our lives, I have selected the gyroscope as a visual representation of this aspect of The RESET Model. A gyroscope is a device for measuring and maintaining orientation based on the principle of conservation of angular momentum. Once spinning, the device tends to resist changes to its orientation due to the angular momentum of the wheel.

More than any other time in history, people today are living increasingly faster and unbalanced lives. As the speed of life increases through technology, change, and increased globalization, we must be more diligent in pursuing, achieving, and maintaining balance. We know that millions of people are seeking a greater sense of balance, as evidenced by the exploding industry of life coaching and wellness consulting. Chances are that you too have struggled to balance the different areas of your life. How often do you feel pulled between meeting your business obligations and being at your child's dance recital or ball game? And how frequently do you opt for fast food instead of a more healthy option as you run from one meeting to another?

My doctoral dissertation work focused on the topic of life balance as it specifically related to the experience of work stress among corporate executives. Research clearly reveals that life balance, or a lack thereof, has a direct and predictable impact on the presence of work stress. Taking this a step further, one can suppose that if a lack of balance increases work stress, it also may negatively impact other areas of life.

While I consider myself an academic expert in life balance, I confess that living the behaviors that achieve balance is far more complicated. Although I have a vivid understanding of the importance of balance, it's often challenging to climb out of bed and leave for the gym for an early morning workout or slow down in the middle of the day for a healthy lunch choice instead of opting for a quick drive-through meal.

Though I clearly understand the importance of balance, like you, I struggle daily with actually applying it to my life. After years of focus and study in this area, my own life balance has improved significantly through the use of the methodology that is part of The RESET Model. Likewise, many whom I have coached and counseled through the years have experienced significant increases in overall balance, which gave them a sense of greater control and strength to achieve their goals and dreams.

I am inspired by the perseverance and commitment of individuals like Chad Hymas and Nick Vulicic, who live with incredible deficits yet still do not let their challenges hold them back from creating and living a life of purpose with passion. Chad was involved in a serious accident on April 3, 2001, which resulted in him being rendered a quadriplegic. Nick was born into the world with what many would consider to be insurmountable obstacles — no arms and no legs. While at first glance it would be reasonable to suppose that each of these men could easily succumb to living the life of a victim of fate or circumstance, both have instead leveraged their challenges to create meaningful lives. They bring hope, healing, education, and passion to literally millions of individuals. That is the true essence of RESET and creating balance through all areas of life.

If you are honest with yourself, you most likely are similar to the majority of individuals who are reading this book and with those I have worked with who struggle with life balance. While the desire to change is there, the ability to fully understand how to begin is missing. In the following section, you will develop an awareness of what your current state is with respect to the seven aspects of balance and then begin the journey to formulate a specific plan for living a life of greater balance in the future.

Life Balance: An Overview

The key to keeping your balance is knowing when you've lost it.
Anonymous

The concept of life balance has been explored for decades. It was not until the end of the twentieth century, however, that considerable research began in this important area. These findings have yielded a deeper understanding of the aspects that significantly impact our experience of total wellness.

Abraham Maslow was one of the first to consider the concept of life balance. He viewed balance and wellness as goals to be pursued throughout an individual's life.[1] His model suggests that an individual strives to attain physiological needs at the most basic level, followed by safety, a sense of belonging, esteem, and self-actualization. Maslow concluded that life balance is realized ultimately through the achievement of self-actualization, the pinnacle of existence that is deeply rooted in the spirituality and self-awareness of the individual. [2]

Maslow's Hierarchy of Needs

Dr. Bill Hettler, who founded the National Wellness Institute, developed a theory of life balance and wellness based on six areas of balance.[3] He based this model on the belief that a greater sense of wellness is achieved to the degree that an individual is able to pursue and attain balance in these areas. And Dr. Donald B. Ardell, who is often credited with founding the wellness movement in the United States, developed a five-dimensional model of balance that integrates aspects of environmental awareness, individual meaning, nutritional balance, physical fitness, and stress management.[4]

Based on the theories of Alfred Adler, an Austrian medical doctor, psychotherapist, and founder of the school of individual psychology, another model developed viewing the individual as a "whole" and stressing the fact that the integration of multiple parts into that whole has a critical impact on the individual.[5] This theory creates a holistic model for life balance and wellness. According to the theory, wellness comprises five overarching life balance dimensions—love, work, friendship, self-regulation, and spirituality. This approach helped individuals to establish plans to increase overall wellness and experience a greater sense of health.[6]

All of the preceding models of life balance and wellness were based on the premise of appreciating the wholeness of the individual and on the assumption that the pursuit of life balance will result in an increase in health and wellness. Whether the model is linear or variable, there is a clear understanding that all aspects of life are interconnected and the such connections impact a person in totality.

When it comes to the existing models, one aspect is garnering attention for its impact on life balance. In recent years, we have experienced a cascading failure of financial balance in the United States and global economies as a result of mismanagement of financial resources. As I have worked closely with individuals to bring growth and healing to their lives, I have observed that financial concerns increasingly are a significant cause of stress and life imbalance. Research shows that in the context of personal relationships, financial issues are a leading cause of divorce. Similarly, from a professional standpoint, industry trends suggest that moral, ethical, and legal violations are occurring on individual and corporate levels in the pursuit of greater financial wellness.

Financial balance affects every aspect of our lives and often is a leading filter through which decisions are made. Companies strive to maximize stakeholder value. Likewise, individuals most often seek to maximize their personal financial value. Some individuals do consciously decide to live a life of financial scarcity (consider Mother Teresa). But the vast majority place financial health and prosperity as a core focus. While Dr. Hettler would have included this concept as part of occupational balance (i.e., the extent to which one's job or career provides the opportunity to earn in a way that is satisfying for the individual), I believe that this aspect of life is so pivotal that it demands self-evaluation and its own set of goals.

I believe there are seven areas of life balance that are essential to understanding, evaluating, and establishing goals to enhance life for every individual and that these areas are critical in providing the stability essential for achieving success.

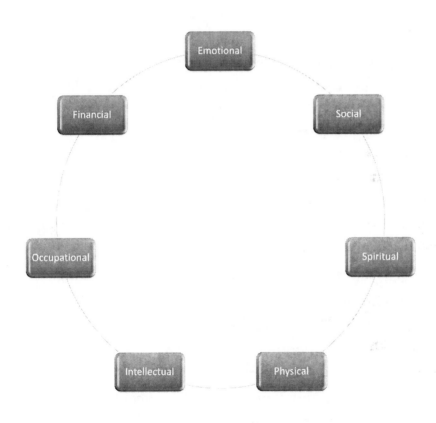

Aspects of Balance

Aspects of Balance

Emotional Aspect

The first aspect of life balance is emotional wellness. Best defined as awareness and acceptance of an individual's feelings, this aspect is characterized by the extent that one is positive and enthusiastic about life. The ability to manage feelings, deal with stress, maintain positive relationships, and arrive at decisions through a combination of thoughts, feelings, philosophies, and behaviors is evidence of strong emotional wellness. Awareness of emotions leads to healthy behaviors that in turn build a stronger sense of community.[7] Ultimately, emotional wellness is based on the awareness and acceptance of feelings and the ability to maintain an optimistic life view.[8]

Emotional wellness involves being aware of the feelings that are in us and the feelings of others. The greatest sense of emotional wellness is experienced when we are able to view our feelings as positive and affirming. People who are emotionally well can accept their feelings as being part of them and avoid judgmental attitudes and behaviors that would seek only to minimize the importance of those emotions. Although emotional wellness is clearly focused on the individual, it is important to remember that at its core, emotional wellness is the ability of people to understand themselves and their feelings and to use and manage emotions effectively for the benefit of themselves and others. For example, people who frequently lose their temper and, as a result, lose control of their behavior could be said to have low emotional wellness. By contrast, people who understand where their emotions come from, use their emotions to their advantage to make a positive difference for others, and are able to modify their behavior for positive outcomes could be said to have high emotional wellness.

As we go through life, the experiences we enjoy that are highlighted with increased emotion are often those that we remember most. We have all experienced times when a smell, a song, a sound, or an image we see immediately transports us back in time to an event that remains so vivid in our minds that it was like it happened yesterday. Those times were moments of RESET in our lives. They set us on a new course with a newly defined and experienced emotion that built on the person we were.

Do you remember your first kiss? That experience, for many, was a life-changing moment. For me this happened when I was in third grade and living in Tifton, Georgia. Although we only lived there for about a year and a half, I met the love of my life shortly after we moved to town. Her name was Nancy, and to an eight-year-old boy, she was the most beautiful thing I had ever seen. I still remember her long blond hair and how we would play tag on the playground during recess. Having moved from "up north," I was new to the area, and she was a caring and compassionate person who made me feel like a member of her family and not a stranger. Unfortunately, our time together was cut short due to my dad's job change. As my family made the final preparations to move back to Indiana, Nancy and I met at the side of the apartment we were living in to say our final good-byes. As I reached out to give her a hug, she surprised me by giving me a kiss on the cheek. I remember seeing fireworks and running in circles around a tall pine tree as I was overcome with feelings of "love" for my elementary school sweetheart. For a little boy and his "girlfriend," this was an innocent experience. But from an emotional standpoint, it made a mark that has lasted a lifetime.

What are the moments that you remember from your youth? Most likely these are the experiences that are saturated with such emotion that they have been permanently scripted into your memory.

Our capacity to experience life to the fullest is dependent upon our ability to feel a full range of emotions and bring them into the person we are becoming.

While certainly each of us has different emotional experiences, there are also moments that are filled with emotional energy that we share and that shape a generation. Throughout history there have been many events such as these, such as the assassination of John F. Kennedy and Martin Luther King, the space shuttle Challenger tragedy, the massacre of the defenseless children and teachers at Columbine, Hurricane Katrina, and the financial crisis at the end of the first decade of 2000. All of these events were shared by the nation, either personally or though the study of history, and had a unique impact on each of us as individuals.

Perhaps no single event, however, has impacted the current generation more than the terror attacks of September 11, 2001. The tragedy caused a radical shift in the perception of the greatest nation on the plant and resulted in a significant change in the quality of life of the citizens of the United States. We most likely can all remember the moment we first became aware of the events of that fateful day. We shared an experience and watched in horror as the media reported on the events that unfolded throughout the day. I vividly remember the feelings of incredible sadness, anger, and disbelief I had when I watched the images of New Yorkers walking through the streets, covered in gray ash from the destroyed World Trade Center towers. For that day and for weeks, months, and years to follow, we worked individually and as a nation to bring sense to the events and gain a greater emotional perspective. Tragedy of any type has the effect of bringing us to a place of self-reflection and often to a point of choice where we can either become stuck in an emotional prison or grow from the experience and become stronger and even better able to confront similar situations in the future.

Emotional wellness gives people the ability to enjoy the highs of life and not become overwhelmed when challenges and obstacles arise. It is founded on an appreciation for the value of self and a connection with others. A positive mental image and attitude are often experienced through emotional wellness, as is the ability to understand and express one's feelings honestly, clearly, and authentically. Emotional wellness has been found to be essential for overall wellness and is critical as a foundation for success.[9] The following assessment will help you to determine your degree of emotional wellness.

Emotional Wellness Assessment

The emotional aspect of balance involves recognizing, accepting and taking responsibility for your feelings. Read each statement carefully and respond honestly by using the following scoring:

Strongly Agree   4 Points
Agree   3 Points
Disagree   2 Points
Strongly Disagree   1 Point

2	I feel positive about myself and my life.
3	I am able to form and maintain strong personal relationships.
2	I am able to be the person that I choose to be and accept responsibility for my actions.
4	I believe that challenges and change are opportunities for personal growth.
2	I believe that I am performing to the best of my ability and that I am living my greatest potential.
2	I understand and can adjust to life's ups and down effectively.
2	I appropriately cope with stress and make time for activities that provide an opportunity for me to rest, relax, and recharge.
3	I am able to recognize and express my feelings effectively.
3	I am non-judgmental in my approach to others.
2	I love life and enjoy making the most of each day.
25	**Total for Emotional Wellness Aspect**

Score: **32-40 Points** – This aspect is a great strength for you and most likely is a source of satisfaction and stability in your life.

Score: **19-32 Points** – While not an immediate issue, there is opportunity to improve in this area.

Score: **10-18 Points** - This aspect is an issue for you and requires dedicated focus to avoid creating imbalance overall in your life.

A full version of this assessment that is suitable for copy is located in the "Assessments of Balance" section at the end of this book.

Social Aspect

The second aspect of life balance is social wellness. This aspect focuses on the importance of individual engagement in the social environment and community of living. Wellness begins through an awareness of our interrelatedness and the support that is available through others. Achieving a sense of harmony and thinking first of the needs of others are foundational to the social aspect of wellness.[10]

Social wellness is the ability to understand and effectively navigate the complexities of social relationships between people. This requires the ability of the individual to effectively interpret social situations and appreciate the importance of the individual in the context of the larger picture of multiple individuals. The ability to understand the environment in which the person is currently placed and the dynamics that are at play is essential.

In the context of the work environment, it is widely understood that office politics are a way of life. While there may be differences from one company to another, the reality remains that when multiple individuals are brought together in a single area to work toward a common goal, negotiations and the positioning of people will result. An individual with high social wellness will have the ability to effectively interpret the political waters of an organization and manage the relationships that are present in a way that creates the most positive working environment possible while accomplishing the required results.

An understanding of social situations is an integral aspect of social wellness, as are a desire and ability to engage in such situations. Being an active and contributing member of society is essential for wellness. We are all social creatures. Our ability to develop a strong sense of self within the context of our relationships with others requires the ability to self-reflect, understand individual motives and emotions, recognize the social factors that impact us, and realize that the way we make decisions and act are influenced by people around us.[11]

How we build and experience social wellness has changed significantly over the years. I vividly remember how important spending personal time together was to my family when I was living at home in Lebanon, Indiana. One of the non-negotiables in our home was family dinner. My mom would begin working to prepare the evening meal late in the afternoon, and it seemed that it was always ready right before my dad arrived home from work. We each had our place to sit at the table, and there was an implied social structure to the experience. Dad would talk about his day first, and then my brother and I would do the same. Mom would often share as well, but in retrospect I understand that as a stay-at-home mom, her desire to engage with our worlds was realized through hearing about our days and living those experiences with us through our stories. What I remember most as I reflect back on those times was the laughter. It was not as much about the meal as it was about the deepening of our relationships with each other.

For many today, the family dinner is no longer on the menu. We move so quickly from one responsibility and priority to another that the opportunity to slow down, connect, and share our lives with each other is quickly evaporating. Even when we do devote time to eating dinner together, boundaries need to be reinforced to avoid the interruptions of text messaging, Facebook posts, phone calls, and Tweets. Though we are more connected than ever before, there has never been a time when we have felt more isolated and alone.

The connection of people that has been facilitated through the development of communication technology has been truly magnificent. With the type press in the late 1800s, we were first able to obtain stories and messages from around the world. In the late 1930s, television began to emerge as a more viable means of obtaining information. While the visual messaging that was available through this new medium of communication was more regional in nature, it provided an opportunity to gain insight into others and experience a growing sense of community.

Through the years, as technology increased, the opportunity to receive video from around the world became part of daily life. We could enjoy the world news each evening as our global community that was once out of reach became even smaller. With the invention of the Internet and development of social media, global connection has moved from being one of awareness, or one-way, to interactive, or multidirectional. The Internet has been a catalyst for allowing us to live and actively participate in a truly global community. As a teen I had a pen pal from Korea. We would write letters to each other and engage in conversation that would take weeks or months to complete. Today, through the use of e-mail, text messaging, affordable global phone services, and various social media platforms (such as Facebook, Twitter, LinkedIn, Google+, YouTube, Vimeo, and Pinterest), connecting to others around the world has become instantaneous, ultimately bringing us closer together through an increased understanding of and appreciation for the differences we share.

Social wellness gives individuals the ability to effectively understand and relate to others as engaged and contributing members of society. In reality, we all experience different social environments that require potentially different abilities from a social standpoint to be successful. Our social paradigm can change as we go from employee to family member to friend to community volunteer. In the end, it is our ability to understand the social dynamics, to engage as an active member in each of those settings, and to adapt appropriately that results in the greatest sense of social wellness. The following assessment will help you to determine your degree of social wellness.

Social Wellness Assessment

The social aspect of balance involves developing, nourishing and encouraging satisfying relationships. Read each statement carefully and respond honestly by using the following scoring:

Strongly Agree 4 Points
Agree 3 Points
Disagree 2 Points
Strongly Disagree 1 Point

Score	Statement
4	I have at least one person in my life who I consider a great confidant and best friend.
2	My relationships with my family are positive and uplifting.
3	I am able to develop close, personal relationships.
3	I am interested in others, including those who have different backgrounds and experiences from me.
2	I am involved in activities in my local community where I volunteer and serve others.
3	I have an awareness of other's needs and help others when possible.
3	I do something for fun and just for myself at least once a week.
2	I am able to effectively balance my needs with the needs of others.
3	I enjoy spending time with others and am able to develop a personal connection with others.
2	I place value on relationships and strive daily to improve relationships with those in my life.
27	**Total for Social Wellness Aspect**

Score: **32-40 Points** – This aspect is a great strength for you and most likely is a source of satisfaction and stability in your life.

Score: **19-32 Points** – While not an immediate issue, there is opportunity to improve in this area.

Score: **10-18 Points** - This aspect is an issue for you and requires dedicated focus to avoid creating imbalance overall in your life.

A full version of this assessment that is suitable for copy is located in the "Assessments of Balance" section at the end of this book.

Spiritual Aspect

A third aspect of life balance is spiritual wellness. This aspect seeks to ascribe meaning to human existence and helps us realize that humans are just one small piece of a larger system. Achieving a sense of peace and joy and connecting to the broader aspects of existence are goals for spiritual wellness. The exploration of the meaning of life, the development of an appreciation for the different beliefs of others, and the pursuit of a life of harmony with oneself are core values of the area of spiritual health.[12]

Spiritual wellness is a very personal and private experience for many. It involves the exploration and pursuit of a life of alignment where personal values and daily actions coincide, resulting in consistency between the core of the individual and actions. It is a personal awareness of the uniqueness of life and the special place we have in creation. For many, the journey to spiritual wellness comes during times of quiet introspection, when the vastness of the world and universe intersects with the essence of humanity. If you have never done so, I encourage you now to meditate on the following images:

The ocean: See the vastness of the sea in your mind's eye. Hear the sound of the surf as it breaks on the shore. Consider the complexity of the ocean ecosystem, where millions of species of plant and marine life live.

The mountains: See the immensity of the Rocky Mountains, the Grand Canyon, the Himalayas, and Mount Everest. Consider the power required to form such magnificent natural wonders.

The sunset: See the evening sun as it sets on the horizon. Imagine the vibrant colors of the setting sun as it sinks for another day beyond our point of view to usher in a night sky filled with billions of stars that comprise our solar system and are visible to us from Earth.

New York City: See the buildings, the infrastructure, the work of man's hand to create the marvels of modern engineering. See the lights. Hear the sounds of rushing cars, subways, and people passing by. Consider the ideas, planning, preparation, and work that were invested to create the largest city in the United States.

It is important to remember that spiritual wellness is not focused on religious precepts or doctrines, although certainly religious expression could be a part of a life of spiritual wellness. Instead, it is concerned with viewing the self in the context of a greater realm of reality and developing a personal and powerful sense of one's place in overall existence.

A second aspect of spiritual wellness is a personal sense of purpose and awareness of one's reason for living. Each of us has a role to play in the theater of life, and developing an understanding of that role, as well as an ability to embrace the importance and value of one's life, will lead to a greater sense of connection and clarity of purpose. It is through our personal understanding of our purpose for living that we can embrace our spiritual journey.

Spiritual wellness is a lifelong process of self-discovery and revelation. Spiritual awareness comes through a constant and focused attention toward understanding one's own beliefs and growth, a process that can be likened to the peeling of an onion. Children often accept and adopt the spiritual values that are modeled by their parents. Teens begin to develop an increased awareness of self, which often manifests in a direct rejection of anything related to their parents in an effort to begin to develop a personal identity that is separate from the family. In early adulthood, a balance begins to develop where personal beliefs are reconciled with those that were foundational in the childhood years and learned from the parents. This reconciliation allows for the ability to establish a foundation upon which a continued lifelong journey toward understanding self is achieved.

Spiritual discovery often comes when we are calm and open. Through the quieting of our thoughts, a broader understanding will emerge. Many years ago I began the process of journaling. It has been an incredible experience for me and has helped me on my own journey of spiritual wellness, which I continue to pursue. Even today, I can return to the writings of years ago, ponder what I was experiencing at that time, and consider how my understanding of self, others, and my place in creation has developed. Each person is unique and should answer the question, "What do I do to connect to the spiritual nature of my experience?"

Spiritual wellness is an essential aspect of overall life balance. Developing a strong sense of self, understanding personal values, and determining how those provide direction in life are essential. This understanding will then lead to an increased clarity of purpose that will provide a foundation upon which to grow. The following assessment will help you to determine your degree of spiritual wellness.

Spiritual Wellness Assessment

The spiritual aspect of balance involves seeking meaning and purpose in one's life. Read each statement carefully and respond honestly by using the following scoring:

Strongly Agree	4 Points
Agree	3 Points
Disagree	2 Points
Strongly Disagree	1 Point

	I have a clear understanding of the purpose of my life and the reason that I am living.
	The goals and activities that I engage are consistent with my purpose.
	I am comfortable with my spiritual life.
	I live my life in alignment between my values and my daily actions.
	I engage consistently in times of prayer, meditation, or quiet personal reflection.
	When I am feeling overwhelmed or depressed, my spiritual life is a source of direction and inspiration for me.
	I am willing to consider new and different ideas even if they do not make sense to me initially.
	I am optimistic about life and seek to live my life in self-affirming ways.
	I am able to forgive others easily for wrongs that have been committed against me.
	I am able to forgive myself easily for wrongs that I have committed against others.
	Total for Spiritual Wellness Aspect

Score: **32-40 Points** – This aspect is a great strength for you and most likely is a source of satisfaction and stability in your life.

Score: **19-32 Points** – While not an immediate issue, there is opportunity to improve in this area.

Score: **10-18 Points** - This aspect is an issue for you and requires dedicated focus to avoid creating imbalance overall in your life.

A full version of this assessment that is suitable for copy is located in the "Assessments of Balance" section at the end of this book.

Physical Aspect

Physical wellness, the fourth aspect to be considered, involves regular physical exercise, a healthy diet, adequate rest, and the avoidance of substances that would lead to decreased physical health (e.g., tobacco, drugs, and excessive alcohol). Physical health leads to the ability to participate actively in all areas of life, and those who work to ensure their own physical wellness realize the importance of preventative as well as curative interventions. Foundational to this concept are the tenets of healthy eating and physical fitness for healthy living.[13]

There are three areas to consider when thinking about physical health: nutrition, rest, and exercise. According to the website http://www.HealthGuidance.org, nutrition is "the sum total of the processes involved in the taking in and the utilization of food substances by which growth, repair, and maintenance of the body are accomplished."[14] Our bodies were created with certain dietary and nutritional needs for normal and healthy functioning. A steady diet of any one food can lead to the body being challenged when it comes to operating with maximum efficiency. Remedy Health Media, LLC suggests that healthy nutrition can be achieved by following three steps. First, eat a wide variety of foods. Second, remember that fruits, vegetables, grains, and legumes (foods high in complex carbohydrates, fiber, vitamins, and minerals, low in fat, and free of cholesterol) should make up the bulk of the calories consumed. And third, maintain a balance between calorie intake and calorie expenditure.[15]

Rest is the second aspect of physical health. In our fast-paced world, people often find it difficult to set time aside for rest throughout the day, let alone to prioritize a night of good sleep. Considerable research has been conducted regarding the most appropriate amount of sleep by age group. Research suggests that infants require the most at between twelve to eighteen hours of sleep per day. This amount decreases throughout our lives but should never be less than approximately eight hours per day. The National Sleep Foundation recommends the following sleep tips:

- Establish consistent sleep and wake schedules, even on weekends.
- Create a regular, relaxing bedtime routine, such as soaking in a hot bath or listening to soothing music, that you begin an hour or more before the time you expect to fall asleep.
- Create a sleep-conducive environment that is dark, quiet, comfortable, and cool.
- Sleep on a comfortable mattress and pillows.
- Use your bedroom only for sleep and sex. Keep "sleep stealers" out of the bedroom, which means you should avoid watching TV, using a computer, or reading in bed.
- Finish eating at least two to three hours before your regular bedtime.
- Exercise regularly during the day or at least a few hours before bedtime.
- Avoid caffeine and alcohol products close to bedtime. Give up smoking.[16]

The third area that is essential for physical wellness is exercise. The Health Discovery Network suggests that there are several benefits for individuals who engage in regular (three to four times a week) exercise.[17] These include prevention of diseases, improved stamina, strengthened and toned body and muscles, enhanced flexibility, weight control, and improved quality of life (reduced stress, enhanced moods, and increased quality of sleep). There are three main categories of exercise. The first is flexibility exercise, which is focused on enhancing movements of muscles and joints. Stretching and bending are the common methods of flexibility training. Next, aerobic exercise, also known as cardiovascular exercise, is designed to strengthen muscles and promote cardiovascular endurance. This type of exercise aims to improve the oxygen intake by the body's cells and involves movement of the muscle groups from a moderate to intense exercise level for an extended period of at least twenty minutes. Examples of aerobic exercise include running, jogging, cycling, swimming, dancing, and playing sports. The third area of exercise is anaerobic exercise, which is focused on building muscles and enhancing their size, strength, and endurance. Some common examples of anaerobic exercise include sit-ups, pull-ups, push-ups, squats, rowing, and weight training.

Childhood and adult obesity, the lethargy of the nation, rising health costs, and lost work productivity due to increasing physical issues are becoming an epidemic. Billions of dollars are spent each year to treat medical conditions that are exacerbated by unhealthy living and unhealthy choices. Similarly, billions of dollars are lost each year by companies in sick time, decreased productivity, work injuries, and other factors that are related to the increased physical decline of the work force. This is an area that must be addressed through education in general and the establishment of personal discipline in each of our lives to pursue greater physical wellness.

I must admit that of all the aspects of balance, maintaining physical wellness is the most challenging for me. I have found that it is the easiest to neglect during a busy day and that I often end up rationalizing my struggle with the belief that "I will start tomorrow." As I reflect back on my journey to increased physical wellness, I can see my greatest stumbling block is doing too much too fast and then burning out. This was fully experienced in all its glory on Monday, January 4, 2010. I had spent great effort to ensure I was properly prepared for the new adventure of committing myself to increasing my physical wellness by running every day. I had done my research by talking with "expert" runners and reading running magazines. I had purchased all of the necessary equipment and prepared my iPod with several instructional programs so I could enrich my emotional, intellectual, and spiritual wellness along with my physical wellness during my morning run. I had believed that I was fully prepared to begin this journey to increased physical wellness.

On the day I had planned to launch my new exercise routine, I got up early and, despite an unusually cold morning, ventured out to begin my commitment to a daily run. My plan on this first day was to walk a quarter of a mile (my warm-up), run a mile, and then walk another quarter mile (my cool down). The first quarter mile in the cold morning air was exhilarating, and I mentally absorbed the words of Jim Rohn that were playing through the iPod. The problems started when I reached the midpoint of my "run phase." It was as if my body had engaged in a full revolt against the idea of running at all. Obviously, despite all of my preparation and research, I had neglected to fully understand or appreciate the importance of starting slow and working up over time. Gasping for breath with my heart beating out of my chest, I remember wondering if I would have the strength to make it back home at all. To make matters worse, my middle son's school bus was coming down the road. While my body said "collapse," I knew I had to muster the strength to at least enter a slow jog as the bus passed so as not to give my teenage son anything else to be embarrassed by his father about in front of his friends. I did finally make it home, and for the next three days, I paid dearly for my overly zealous start to my daily running program.

I am pleased to report that I did eventually return to my daily run, but at a much slower, more intentional pace so I could build up my physical endurance and strength. Ultimately, I have a goal to run the Music City Marathon that is hosted each year in Nashville, Tennessee. While I am confident that my purpose is not to be a world-class athlete, I know that taking appropriate steps to maintain physical wellness to maximize my ability to achieve success is essential. Regardless of where you may be life, it is never too late to start taking steps today toward increased physical wellness. As the old Aesop's Fable says, you must care for the golden goose if you hope to continue to receive the gift of golden eggs.

Physical wellness is an integral component of a life of balance. Caring for your body will allow you the opportunity to live a long and healthy life and more easily realize success. The following assessment will help you to determine your degree of physical wellness.

Physical Wellness Assessment

The physical aspect of balance involves encouraging regular activities that produce endurance, flexibility and strength. Read each statement carefully and respond honestly by using the following scoring:

Strongly Agree   4 Points
Agree   3 Points
Disagree   2 Points
Strongly Disagree   1 Point

Score	Statement
4	I engage in vigorous aerobic exercise for 20 to 30 minutes at least three times a week
4	I make nutrition a priority and eat fruits, vegetables, and whole grains every day.
4	I do not engage in the use of tobacco products.
4	I consciously minimize the consumption of cholesterol, dietary fats, and oils.
1	I do not engage in the consumption of alcohol or limit myself to no more than one drink per day.
2	I get the appropriate amount of sleep for my age and wake in the morning feeling rested and refreshed.
4	I make good choices regarding my safety including wearing a seat belt and avoiding texting when driving.
2	I am able to effectively manage stress in my life.
3	I put a high priority on my health by staying current on medical and dental examinations, immunizations, and visit the doctor if issues arise.
3	I maintain an appropriate and consistent (avoiding extremes) weight for my age and body composition.
31	**Total for Physical Wellness Aspect**

Score: **32-40 Points** – This aspect is a great strength for you and most likely is a source of satisfaction and stability in your life.

Score: **19-32 Points** – While not an immediate issue, there is opportunity to improve in this area.

Score: **10-18 Points** - This aspect is an issue for you and requires dedicated focus to avoid creating imbalance overall in your life.

A full version of this assessment that is suitable for copy is located in the "Assessments of Balance" section at the end of this book.

Intellectual Aspect

Intellectual wellness involves the mental activities and creative processes of the individual. Through the expansion of knowledge and skill, we are afforded the ability to share what we have learned with others. Problem solving, creativity, and developing oneself are hallmarks of intellectual health and can be manifested through reading, engaging in lively dialogue, and developing intellectual curiosity. Central tenets of this dimension of wellness include the pursuit of intellectual and creative endeavors that enhance self-satisfaction and the ability to be productive, to problem solve, and to use the mental resources that are available to us.[18]

Since we are complex individuals, the concept of intelligence is also varied and complex. With this model of intellectual wellness, the focus is on the development of the cognitive and creative aspects of intelligence. Cognitive intelligence is the ability to learn and understand. It could best be described as the traditional IQ, which involves the ability to understand through logic and reason and to demonstrate strength in reading, writing, analyzing, and prioritizing. At the core of cognitive intelligence is a desire to learn, develop oneself, and engage in activities that are intellectually stimulating. Through this learning and growth comes the ability to link concepts and ideas together and present thoughts that are cogent and compelling. Individuals who demonstrate high attention toward the development of intellectual wellness are discerning and discriminating regarding the information that they allow to enter their conscious mind. They realize that mental development is highly influenced by the input that they allow to come into their perceptions and thoughts.

There is also a creative aspect of intellectual wellness whereby an individual gravitates toward actives that allow the ability to generate new thoughts and explore the abstract nature of life.

Individuals with high intellectual wellness often enjoy immersing themselves into the world of literature and mentally stimulating activities and have a deep appreciation for the arts. There is a desire to synthesize existing information and ideas into new concepts and take unique approaches to problem solving. This area also involves the ability to bring forth new ideas and create novel associations. Individuals who are high in creative intelligence often engage in activities that enable them to design, form, and build new thoughts, concepts, and ideas from scratch. They look for connections that then lead to new and innovative expressions.

At no other time in history has the opportunity for intellectual growth been greater than it is today. With access to the Internet, the world's wealth of information is literally at our fingertips. Through a quick search, we can find information on virtually any topic imaginable for essentially no cost. In addition, with the growth of distance learning and flexible education systems, barriers that used to exist with school scheduling that would prevent individuals with full-time jobs from returning to pursue their education are removed. The flexibility that is created through technology and new learning systems has removed obstacles to learning and granted access for all. Anyone who has a desire to invest in themselves to learn and grow can accomplish that desire.

Likewise, there is no other time when distractions to intellectual growth have been greater. Such growth requires commitment, stamina, and determination to forego a favorite show, turn off the television, and instead open a book. It is a daily discipline that grows into a habit that allows learning and intellectual growth to be a part of our lives.

Intellectual wellness is invaluable in creating and sustaining a life of balance. When viewed through the lens of the two core aspects that comprise overall intelligence—cognitive and creative—it is clear that it is critical for an individual to develop this area to be effective

90

in all other areas of life. The ability to think, reason, interpret, synthesize, and create is foundational to intellectual wellness. The following assessment will help you to determine your degree of intellectual wellness.

Intellectual Wellness Assessment

The intellectual aspect of balance involves embracing creativity and mental stimulation.   Read each statement carefully and respond honestly by using the following scoring:

Strongly Agree	4 Points
Agree	3 Points
Disagree	2 Points
Strongly Disagree	1 Point

	I am interested in learning just for the joy of learning.
	I believe that my education has prepared me for what I would like to accomplish in life.
	I enjoy sharing with others the things that I have learned.
	I am selective in how I spend my time and avoid activities that would be mentally stagnating.
	I am able to analyze, synthesize, and evaluate multiple aspects of a discussion or issue.
	I am interested in the viewpoint of others, even if it is different from my own.
	I am motivated to learn and improve myself.
	I enjoy reading a variety of materials and am consistently spending time in this activity.
	I understand the importance of personal continuous improvement and actively participate in activities that challenge me to grow.
	I seek opportunities to keep informed of current affairs locally, nationally, and internationally.
	Total for Intellectual Wellness Aspect

Score: **32-40 Points** – This aspect is a great strength for you and most likely is a source of satisfaction and stability in your life.

Score: **19-32 Points** – While not an immediate issue, there is opportunity to improve in this area.

Score: **10-18 Points** - This aspect is an issue for you and requires dedicated focus to avoid creating imbalance overall in your life.

A full version of this assessment that is suitable for copy is located in the "Assessments of Balance" section at the end of this book.

Occupational Aspect

The sixth aspect of balance is occupational wellness. This aspect focuses on the personal satisfaction achieved through life work and the attitude maintained about that work. People's ability to use their unique gifts, skills, and talents is foundational to occupational wellness. That ability helps to encourage the pursuit of a career that is personally meaningful and engaging and allows active participation in the world of work and surrounding community.[19]

Occupational wellness ultimately is achieved when you select a career, job, or life work that is rewarding and enjoyable. It is important to remember that the concepts of "rewarding" and "enjoyable" are different for each individual. For example, some find great fulfillment and satisfaction in careers that enable them to work outdoors, while others prefer to work in an indoor environment. Some find enjoyment in work that lets them talk and interact with a variety of people, while others prefer to work alone in a quieter environment on activities that require deep concentration. It also is important to remember that "work" is not limited to occupational endeavors that are external to the home; instead, it encompasses all areas of life. For example, mothers or fathers who decide to devote their life's work to raising their children are just as involved in an occupational endeavor as individuals who have a career external to the home. Wellness in this area is evaluated by a personal sense of happiness with a career choice and a feeling of anticipation toward engaging in work activities. Although many factors impact an overall feeling of happiness, those who wake up every morning with hopeful optimism for the contributions they will make that day at work experience higher levels of occupational wellness.

Another consideration is the alignment of work with personal values. Although some may believe that compartmentalization of life is possible (i.e. work, personal, spiritual, family, etc.), in reality, all areas of life are interrelated. There are core values that we individually hold that are foundational to who we are and provide the basis for the way that we view the world, make decisions, and interpret our circumstances. When our work does not align with our values, frustration can result, leading to decreased overall wellness. It is important to devote time and effort to a process of self-exploration to identify the aspects that are most important to you as a person and then strive to identify career options that are most closely aligned with those values. During my work with individuals from various fields, I have found that those who have the greatest sense of personal values and have worked in roles and companies that allow for the expression of those values experience the highest levels of satisfaction and happiness. I often use assessments such as the Strong Interest Inventory, Self-Directed Search, Myers-Briggs Type Indicator, DiSC, or ProfileXT, just to name a few, combined with a variety of coaching methodologies to help individuals understand themselves more completely and embark on a career path that has the potential of providing the greatest sense of satisfaction.

A third area of this aspect of life balance is the ability to experience a sense of making a difference and the opportunity to contribute at a higher level toward a shared vision. Maslow noted that individuals have a basic need to provide for the physiological needs of life (food, water, shelter, and clothing) and to experience a sense of safety and security. Beyond these basic provisions, they have a desire to pursue experiences that allow for a sense of belonging, build personal esteem, and ultimately help them achieve self-actualization. Self-actualized individuals are those who have experienced the greatest sense of personal growth and have achieved their true potential. In the context of occupational wellness, self-actualized individuals are those who continually are pursuing personal growth and are living up to their greatest potential every day. Once again, there is not a universal standard or ultimate achievement to be sought. Each person is unique and experiences self-actualization in different forms.

The world of work has changed through the decades. In the early to mid twentieth century, individuals would find a job and, outside of drastic circumstances, could expect to remain there until retirement. Today's research shows that the average length of time someone stays in a position is approximately two years. In addition, the number of distinct careers that the average person has in the course of his or her lifetime is seven. While there may be debate on the actual number, it is universally accepted that the number of job changes is on the rise and the longevity with an employer is on the decline. All this means that individuals are seeking more than ever those aspects of their chosen career that bring satisfaction and fulfillment.

Occupational wellness is a core aspect of overall life balance. Each of us has a responsibility to assess the degree to which we feel we are happy and fulfilled with our work, the extent to which we experience satisfaction, and the opportunity we have to self-actualize. The following assessment will help you to determine your degree of occupational wellness.

Occupational Wellness Assessment

The occupational aspect of balance involves choosing a career/job that is rewarding and enjoyable. Read each statement carefully and respond honestly by using the following scoring:

Strongly Agree 4 Point
Agree 3 Points
Disagree 2 Points
Strongly Disagree 1 Point

	I am happy with the choice I made in my career.
	I enjoy my work and experience fulfillment in what I do.
	The responsibilities I have in my job are consistent with my personal values.
	The rewards that are available in my job are consistent with my personal values.
	I am satisfied with the balance I am able to maintain between my professional and personal time.
	I am content with the degree of autonomy and control that I have in my current occupation.
	The work that I do provides a sense of personal satisfaction and motivation.
	I am satisfied with the growth potential that I have in my job and can see opportunities to develop in the future.
	I believe I am able to make a difference through the work I do.
	Overall, my job contributes to my personal and professional well-being.
	Total for Occupational Wellness Aspect

Score: **32-40 Points** – This aspect is a great strength for you and most likely is a source of satisfaction and stability in your life.

Score: **19-32 Points** – While not an immediate issue, there is opportunity to improve in this area.

Score: **10-18 Points** - This aspect is an issue for you and requires dedicated focus to avoid creating imbalance overall in your life.

A full version of this assessment that is suitable for copy is located in the "Assessments of Balance" section at the end of this book.

Financial Aspect

The financial aspect is the final area of consideration in life balance. Financial matters are core aspects of our lives. As part of the economic community, we work in a seemingly endless variety of jobs that allow us to earn money, which in turn allows us to create and maintain a certain lifestyle that is in alignment with our personal values and desires. Dave Ramsey suggests that money is both active and amoral.[20] Money is active in that it is always changing. If we consider the economic challenges that pervaded the financial and mortgage markets from 2009 to 2011, it is clear that, as Ramsey states, "Time, interest rates, amounts, cash flows, inflation, recession, and risk all intermingle to create a current that is ever flowing"[21] and unpredictable. Money is amoral in that it is neither good nor bad. Ultimately, it is what we do with money that creates meaning. As a result, included in this aspect are the concepts of how you view money and financial resources, how you manage money on a daily basis, and how you are positioned financially for the future.

We all have different perspectives on money. Some view it as a central focus in life, where the main goal is to gain as much as possible, as fast as possible. Others view finances as a constant source of frustration, where the income never matches the outflow and the ability to achieve financial goals seems ever out of reach. Still others have a healthy concept of money as a means to an end. There is a realization that money is an essential part of life, but not the meaning of life and not the measure of success. Money provides the opportunity to live, and it is a clear understanding of what "living" means that puts financial wellness in the right light and perspective.

The next aspect of financial wellness, once the foundational goals surrounding finances have been established, is to develop a short-term and long-term vision of how finances will be managed and developed. Although each individual may have different goals and objectives, there are two main considerations that must be explored in order to realize those goals. First, people must ask themselves what they are doing today with money to allow them to live in the present, and second, they must ask what they are doing today with money to allow them to live in the future. The first area can encompass a number of areas of financial decision-making, from the type of job they have, to the process they use for budgeting, to how much they save, and their view on credit. Establishing boundaries so that they live within their means and do not spend what they do not have ultimately leads to the greatest sense of financial wellness in the short-term and eliminates the stress that can arise when faced when debt collectors call or foreclosure notices are served.

The second area is focused on making decisions for five years from now through retirement. According to the United States Department of Labor, upon retirement your expenses will be approximately 80 to 90 percent of your pre-retirement expenses.[22] It is then estimated that you will need approximately thirty times your retirement expenses in net worth to be able to maintain your desired standard of living.[23] So if you anticipate that your post-retirement expenses would be approximately fifty thousand dollars per year, you should have one and a half million dollars available as you enter this season of life.

In mid-2008 through late 2010, the United States in particular and the global financial community in general experienced one of the greatest financial crises of our generation. Mortgage loans went into default at record rates, which had an impact on the entire financial landscape. Major industries like manufacturing, construction, and retail suffered the most. Individual saving and investment took the largest hit in decades, forcing in people who had planned to retire at a certain time to remain working due to evaporated financial resources. The dreams of a nation fell apart, and the once seemingly indestructible United States stumbled under the financial pressure. This ultimately resulted in the realization by many of the importance of living within their means. The marker was called on the extravagant lifestyle spending of the early 2000s. While financial stability is increasing, there are lasting implications from the events at the end of the first decade of the twenty-first century. The events brought about a shift in thought on the infallibility of our financial strength as individuals and as a nation.

Financial wellness is essential to obtaining and maintaining an overall sense of life balance. Many individuals take a passive view of this aspect of balance and thereby become a victim of circumstances upon realizing that money is active and the decisions of some can impact all. Wellness in this area comes first by having a clear understanding of the role of money in your life. From this point, approaches can be developed regarding how to make decisions for the short-term and long-term that will enable you to achieve your financial goals and objectives. The following assessment will help you to determine your degree of financial wellness.

Financial Wellness Assessment

The financial aspect of balance involves having an understanding of your financial goals and the short and long-term plans to achieve your financial objectives. Read each statement carefully and respond honestly by using the following scoring:

Strongly Agree 4 Points
Agree 3 Points
Disagree 2 Points
Strongly Disagree 1 Point

	I have a clear understanding of my financial goals and have a healthy view of money.
	I experience little stress when it comes to money or financial matters.
	I balance my financial accounts regularly.
	I know how much debt I currently have.
	I know how much my assets are worth.
	I know my current net worth.
	I know how much money I need to maintain the standard of living that is important to me at the time I retire.
	I have a retirement account and know how the current value of that account.
	I make planning and saving for retirement a financial priority in my life.
	I have a definite plan for retirement and hold myself and my family accountable to that plan.
	Total for Financial Wellness Aspect

Score: **32-40 Points** – This aspect is a great strength for you and most likely is a source of satisfaction and stability in your life.

Score: **19-32 Points** – While not an immediate issue, there is opportunity to improve in this area.

Score: **10-18 Points** - This aspect is an issue for you and requires dedicated focus to avoid creating imbalance overall in your life.

A full version of this assessment that is suitable for copy is located in the "Assessments of Balance" section at the end of this book.

Picture of Balance

Within the context of "seek first to understand," you have completed the process of self-assessment in the seven areas of life balance. From this process you now have a score based on your own evaluation. You should write those individual scores into the following table to give initial insight into your overall degree of balance.

Aspect of Balance	Score
Emotional	
Social	
Spiritual	
Physical	
Intellectual	
Occupational	
Financial	

While the process of aggregating your assessment scores is valuable, I encourage you to take the process one step further. As previously discussed, ultimate stability and strength are achieved to the extent that these seven aspects are in balance. Going back to the gyroscope analogy, the center component of the gyroscope, also called the "rotator," spins at a high rate of speed to prevent the gyroscope from tipping and losing stability. If, however, the rotator is out of balance, the ability to achieve and maintain that stability is compromised.

With this in mind, use the following circular model to draw a line for each of the aspects of life balance that represent your personal score on the assessment. For example, when considering emotional wellness, if your score is thirty, draw a line from the thirty on the right side to the thirty on the left side of the emotional segment of the model. Do this now for each of the seven aspects of balance. A sample of how to complete this process is also included in the appendices.

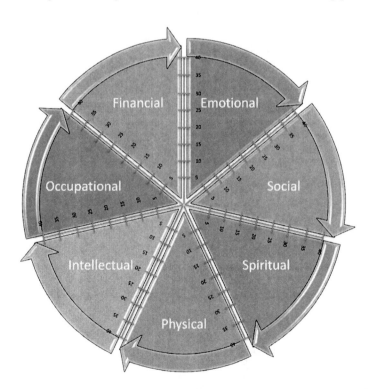

As you complete the exercise, no doubt thoughts and feelings are emerging. Answer the following questions about this experience for you:

1. What are your first impressions of the image that you have drawn?

2. What thoughts emerge for you?

3. What are you feeling at this moment?

4. To what degree do you believe your life is "in balance" today?

Through my work, the personal revelations that naturally come from this exercise include comments such as:

- "Wow, I had no idea!"
- "Finally, this makes sense!"
- "I always knew there were challenges, but I just did not know how to start looking at them."

Regardless of the initial impression, however, invariably each person looks me directly in the eye and with a sense of urgency asks, "Where do I go from here?"

Push RESET on Your Life Balance

When considering the path forward in pushing RESET and achieving a greater sense of balance, it is important to understand first that you are where you are today as a result of choices you have made in your life. Those choices have consequences that manifest in many areas, one of which is the degree of balance that you are experiencing. You have the ability today to begin to make different choices. If you are not happy with your sense of balance, you are in good company! Those who do make balance a core goal in their lives continually evaluate their sense of balance and are disciplined about how they spend their time and energy. Balance is not about perfection; it is about progress one day at a time and maintaining a continual process of self-assessment with modifications as needed to achieve and maintain the greatest sense of balance.

Capitalize on Strengths

When establishing an action plan for achieving a greater sense of balance, first look at the areas of strength for you.

What one or two aspects do you believe you have the highest degree of wellness in?

_____

_____

_____

_____

_____

With these aspects identified, think of one or two actions for each that you can start today that would help you to stay on track with these being areas of strength for you. For example, one area of strength that I consistently maintain is intellectual wellness. I am a passionate learner and teacher, both of which help me maintain intellectual wellness as a high focus area in my life. However, it is not enough to just have an interest in this area; I must also have definite actions that I will take to ensure it remains an area of strength. I set for myself at the beginning of this year the goal of reading on the subjects of change, growth, and success—my core purpose areas—for a minimum of one hour per day. This way I am able to invest in my intellectual growth in my areas of focus for a minimum of 365 hours over the course of the year.

Again, it is critical to not only have actions planned, but also specifics as to what you will do each and every day that will lead to you being able to achieve the results that you have set for yourself. More will be presented on planning and direction regarding the development of goals in the subsequent section. For now, just list a couple of actions that you can take for each of the aspects of balance that you believe are strengths for you today.

Aspect of Balance	Planned Action
_____	1.
	2.
_____	1.
	2.

Mitigate Weaknesses

When considering self-development, we must also look at areas in which we can experience improvement and growth.

What one or two aspects do you believe you have the lowest degree of wellness in?

_____

_____

_____

_____

You will now identify one to two actions for each of these aspects that you could begin today to bring increased wellness to these areas. Though weaknesses are not necessarily bad, they often stand in the way of achieving the greatest degree of success possible. As a result, establishing goals to increase your sense of balance in the areas where wellness is lower helps to mitigate those weaknesses.

As previously mentioned, physical wellness is an area that is not as balanced as I would like for myself. I have established action plans in the areas of healthy eating and daily exercise that have resulted in increased wellness in this area. The actions were not earth-shattering or monumental. From the standpoint of healthy eating, I have given up cookies and milk as a before-bedtime snack in favor of an apple as a healthier option. And as for exercise, I committed to taking a half-mile walk each evening before going to sleep to clear my mind, give thanks for the day, and focus my thoughts on the ultimate goals I have for my life. It is interesting to consider that the act of taking an evening walk with a disciplined focus of thought impacts the physical and emotional aspects of balance, bringing increased wellness to both.

Take time now to identify the two aspects of balance that you would like to RESET with the goal of experiencing a greater sense of wellness and come up with actions that you can start today to have more strength in these areas.

Aspect of Balance	Planned Action
_____	1.
	2.
_____	1.
	2.

Conclusion

Hopefully, through this exploration of the seven aspects of life balance, you have come to an increased understanding that life balance is an essential aspect of success. The personal journey you have begun in this section has no doubt revealed some areas where balance is not as strong as you would like and needs to be addressed. Remember, the way to eat an elephant is one bite at a time. You may have high motivation to move forward with beginning your RESET by establishing goals to "fix" all areas that are out of balance. I caution you, however, to be diligent in your efforts and think carefully about your plans to move forward. If you have a life that is out of balance, remember that it did not occur overnight; it was the product of weeks, months, and years of neglect. Similarly, a life in balance takes time. It requires specific planning and daily discipline to establish habits that are healthy and build balance. It will not happen immediately. By implementing the goals you have established for yourself, you will start to see small, yet measurable results almost immediately.

The goal for beginning today is first to experience a greater sense of balance across all of the seven areas. Once this is achieved, you will turn you attention to building wellness in all areas. This will be developed over time and maintained through diligent effort, discipline, and focus.

As you explore your personal situation, you will also recognize the interconnectedness between these aspects of balance. In my personal situation, this was no more obvious than during the season of life when I returned to pursue my graduate and doctoral degrees. During this seven-year time in my life, I was working in a fulfilling but highly demanding job during the day and then spending approximately six hours each night—and every day on the weekend—immersed in educational endeavors. As a passionate teacher and learner, I found this to be a season of life when I was focused on my intellectual wellness and I grew exponentially, thanks in part to the incredible support of my family. However, it was also during this season that my social wellness with family and friends suffered. Our family spoke openly and often about the challenges that were inherent in working full time and pursuing higher education goals at such an aggressive pace. Through this dialogue, we were able to guard against the natural feelings of resentment, abandonment, and separation. In retrospect, the pursuit of these intellectual endeavors would have been devastating to other aspects of life balance if it had not been for our awareness and understanding of the interconnectedness of all areas of life.

Your desire to experience a RESET and grow in this important area will provide the basis for stability as you continue on your journey to success. We will now turn our focus to the dimension of direction. Rest assured that we will come back to the work that you have done in understanding your current assessment of balance as we work together to establish specific goals to increase the balance in your life.

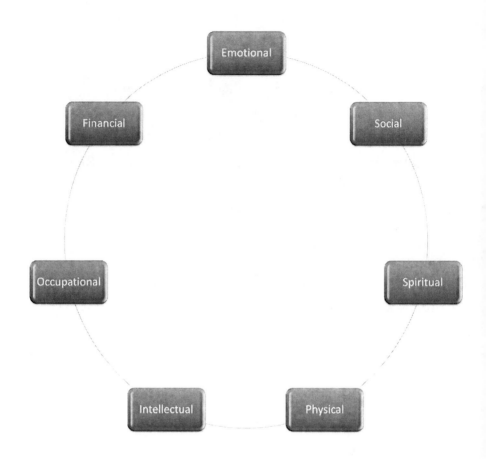

Aspects of Balance

Dimensions of Direction

When doing becomes infused with the timeless quality of being,
that is success.
Eckhart Tolle, author of "The Power of Now"

The difference between can and cannot are only three letters.
Three letters that determine your life's direction.
Remez Sasson, author of "Peace of Mind in Daily Life"

The second element required for achieving a transformational RESET and creating a life of success is direction. On any journey, having a clear understanding of purpose, the energy to attain that purpose, the road map to know which direction you're going, the ability, desire, and fortitude to continue on the journey, and the ability to celebrate the achievement of the destination is essential. This is what life direction is all about.

The compass is the instrument that correlates to this dimension of The RESET Model. A compass is a navigational instrument for finding direction on the Earth. More technically, a compass is a magnetic device that uses a needle to indicate the direction of the magnetic north of a planet's magnetosphere. A compass is only effective and useful if it is able to connect with magnetic north. Without that unwavering pull, a compass needle will just spin and spin and is ultimately useless. Determining the magnetic north that will guide your compass is an integral part of this dimension of The RESET Model.

All too many people are wandering. They are living their lives day in and day out without a clear sense of purpose or direction. This lack of clarity leads to frustration and prevents people from achieving the greatest sense of success possible. They are going through the motions of their lives, and while some seem to be quite successful, they are ultimately unfulfilled. By developing a clear sense of self and clarifying your path to success, you will break through the chains of a life of mediocrity that would seek to hold you back from the full life that is available to you.

As we consider this second element of success, we will be exploring five dimensions that are critical for establishing and maintaining progress and clarity on the journey to success. The first dimension we will explore is that of purpose. At the heart of this aspect of direction is the reason that you are here—more specifically, the reason that you are living. The second dimension we will discuss is that of passion. Passion is the emotional energy that is generated and used for the attainment of a goal. These two dimensions of direction will work together to create the conditions for you to be able to move quickly and unwaveringly down the road toward achieving and realizing the greatest success possible.

The third area is planning. Once you have an understanding of who you are and why you are, your next step is to establish specific plans toward realizing your purpose, full potential, and ultimate success.

We also will be discussing the importance of persisting through the obstacles that we all inevitably face, which is the fourth dimension. At different times during our lives, we will feel pressure and experience obstacles, both internally and externally. The realization that those obstacles exist and our ability to "press on" through those challenges allow us to realize success.

The fifth and final dimension of direction is gratitude. Celebrating your accomplishments is an essential aspect of the journey to success. Though we all work so hard to strive and achieve, we often fail to take time to reflect, remember, and celebrate all of the accomplishments that have been realized on the journey to success.

Bringing together these five dimensions are presented in what I have termed the P⁴G Model, which stands for purpose, passion, planning, persistence, and gratitude. By completely understanding and applying each of these areas in creating and maintaining direction in your life, you will achieve the success you have always dreamed.

Dimensions of Direction

Purpose

Everyone has his own specific vocation or mission in life...Therein he cannot be replaced, nor can his life be repeated. Thus, everyone's task is as unique as is his specific opportunity to implement it.
Victor Frankl, author of "Man's Search for Meaning"

Discerning your purpose involves understanding the reason that you are here. Rick Warren, pastor and author of the highly successful *The Purpose Driven Life*, explored this topic in great detail and developed a forty-day journey to answer the question of the reason we are here and how all the pieces of our lives fit together.[1] It is important to understand, however, that purpose is not about what you do, but rather about who you are. It is about having a deep and unwavering clarity about the reason that you live and the impact that you make.

There is a difference between who you are and what you do. While there certainly may be connections between the two, this is not a necessity. To achieve true success, it is essential that your purpose and your actions are aligned. How many people do you know who seem to have achieved incredible success but ultimately are unfulfilled and still searching for their place in the world? To be able to achieve this first step in life direction, you must remember that what you do follows who you are.

This point became crystal clear to me several years ago, when I was serving as the corporate human resource manager for a multibillion-dollar restaurant company and had to deal with a

114

situation that is as vivid to me today as it was back then. An employee who had been with the organization for approximately ten years was struggling with a variety of work-related performance issues. While he had been a strong performer and great employee throughout the majority of his time with the company, during the previous year he had begun to have significant issues. In particular, he was struggling with his attendance. He often arrived late and asked to leave early and on several occasions called out sick at the last minute. In addition, when he was at work, he continually made mistakes that impacted the productivity and success of his work team. This behavior was creating significant problems for his work team, and he had been counseled on his behavior several times.

On this particular day, after repeated instances of counseling with no change in behavior, the decision was made to end his employment with the company. As I brought this gentleman into my office and delivered the message that his employment was being terminated, his eyes dropped and he placed his head in his hands. After several minutes of silence, he looked up and said, "I understand and appreciate all that you have done for me. Thanks." And then he walked out.

Through the years, my job in human resources had required me to terminate the employment of literally hundreds of people, but this time was different. I was carrying a great burden by not being in a position to help this man more. You see, he had faced some devastating challenges over the previous year. His wife had announced that she had been having an affair for several months and subsequently filed for divorce. His teenage son had been arrested for underage drinking and driving and was now participating in an outpatient recovery program that was mandated by the court system as part of his rehabilitation. And his teenage daughter had announced that she was pregnant. With all of these life circumstances pressing on him, no wonder other areas of his life were affected. Just think back to our previous discussion on life balance, and you can certainly see how all areas of life are interrelated and have an impact on each other.

It was at this time that I had a defining moment and gained complete clarity about my purpose in life. The reason that I was here was not to be a human resource professional—that was simply a means to an end—but to unleash my full potential to make a positive difference in the lives of others. Although I was "successful" as a human resource professional, I was not achieving the highest success, one that aligned with my life purpose and could be lived out in my personal and professional life. This realization was the launching point for my own RESET, which included increased education, professional development, life exploration, and the establishment of a continuing process of self-evaluation focused on realigning those things that I do with who I am. My circumstances did not change overnight—after all, I did have a wife and family to support. However, what did occur was the beginning process of self-exploration, which led to me creating a plan to ultimately be in a position where my purpose would be identically aligned with my passion and actions.

Today, I am blessed to have the opportunity to lead an incredible consulting firm that allows me to use my full potential to make a difference in the lives of individuals and the organization. I have great clarity about my strengths and the value that I bring to my clients. Through this understanding, I have the ability to influence others as an executive, invest in people's lives as a trusted advisor to CEOs and executives in the role of coach and mentor, design and transform the organization as a strategic visionary and leader, and give of myself in the local and regional community by speaking, leading seminars, and volunteering for various organizations.

As I reflect on my career, I realize that there have been times when I was energized, excited, and motivated by my work, but such feelings were often fleeting. As I think about my relationships with my bride and children, I see that there have been times when these relationships were particularly strong and others when there was a greater sense of distance and frustration. However, at this time and in this season, I am authentically living a life of alignment between purpose and actions and can truly say that I am experiencing the greatest sense of fulfillment and happiness than at any other time in my life.

Determination of purpose is not a mystical process, but it does require diligent focus and pursuit. It requires honest exploration and the willingness and ability to answer potentially difficult questions. It requires being open to the possibility of change. It requires the desire to understand yourself in an even deeper way, potentially looking past the life that you created to that which you were created for, and then making the decision to begin charting the course toward alignment between the two.

I have helped many individuals over the years to answer the "tough questions" about themselves and then begin to create a plan for moving forward. It will be amazing to see the transformation that occurs in your life as you embark on the journey toward clarifying your purpose and then slowly, methodically, and thoughtfully begin to change your life situations to align with that purpose.

As part of this process, you will develop:

- Your life mission statement
- Your life vision statement
- Your life values
- Your life purpose statement

Creating these statements to establish awareness of where you are going is a great place to start.

Life Mission Statement

> *The whole secret of a successful life is to find out what is one's destiny to do and then do it.*
> **Henry Ford, inventor and founder of Ford Motor Company**

A life mission statement clearly creates a picture of what you want your life to be and how that aligns with your purpose. A mission statement is not a to-do list, but rather a global expression of who you are and the reason that you are alive. It is important to remember that from the mission statement, clarity of life roles emerge; however, jobs and roles change throughout life's seasons. Purpose, which is inherent in the mission statement, embodies a broad view that encompasses all of your roles.

Mission statements are highly personal. But those with whom you decide to share your mission statement should be able to see your mission lived out in your daily life. Mission statements create observable objectives that are aligned with your purpose and provide the tangible picture of what your life should look like when you live your purpose. Consider the following mission statements of some historic leaders and highly successful organizations:

> The purpose of my life is to humbly serve our Lord by being a loving, playful, powerful, and passionate example of the absolute joy that is available to us the moment that we rejoice in God's gifts and sincerely love and enjoy all his creations.
>
> (Anthony Robbins, self-help author and motivational speaker)

> Let the first act of every morning be to make the following resolve for the day:
> • I shall not fear anyone on Earth.

- I shall fear only God.
- I shall not bear ill will toward anyone.
- I shall not submit to injustice from anyone.
- I shall conquer untruth by truth.
- And in resisting untruth, I shall put up with all suffering.

> (Mahatma Gandhi, preeminent leader of Indian Nationalism)

McDonald's brand mission is to be our customers' favourite place and way to eat and drink. Our worldwide operations are aligned around a global strategy called the Plan to Win, which center on an exceptional customer experience-people, products, place, price, and promotion. We are committed to continuously improving our operations and enhancing our customer's experience.

> (McDonald's)[2]

To unleash the potential and power in people and organizations for the greater good.

> (Ken Blanchard Companies)[3]

To inspire, lift, and provide tools for change and growth of individuals and organizations throughout the world to significantly increase their performance capability in order to achieve worthwhile purposes through understanding and living principle-centered leadership.

> (Stephen R. Covey, author of the highly acclaimed *The 7 Habits of Highly Effective People*)

Google's mission is to organize the world's information and make it universally accessible and useful.

(Google)[4]

The Walt Disney Company's objective is to be one of the world's leading producers and providers of entertainment and information, using its portfolio of brands to differentiate its content, services, and consumer products. The company's primary financial goals are to maximize earnings and cash flow and to allocate capital profitability toward growth initiatives that will drive long-term shareholder value.

(Walt Disney Company)[5]

Life Vision Statement

It is essential that we know our raison d'être.
Dr. Jason Brooks

The vision statement is a concise statement of the unique and distinctive ways that you will accomplish your purpose. It involves taking the mission statement and coming up with actions that align with your overarching purpose. The focus of a vision statement should be to identify and clarify your specific roles and activities and create the framework for living out the mission statement. In addition, a well-crafted vision statement will enhance your ability to maintain laser-like focus on the specific areas where you will achieve your purpose.

As the word "vision" implies, this statement should clearly articulate, in vivid detail, what you are thinking, doing, and feeling. As you begin to consider the vision of your life, close your eyes and develop a picture of yourself at some point in the future. In your mind's eye, picture what you are doing, the people you are with, the accomplishments that you have achieved, and the things that are most important to you. As you develop this vision, take time to reflect on your thoughts and feelings and on how those align with the picture of your future. The creation of a clear image of the future that is consistent with your innate purpose will enable you to begin developing the goals and discipline to bring that vision to life.

Life Values

> *Values are like fingerprints. Nobody's are the same but you leave them all over everything you do.*
> **Elvis Presley**

Values are those core aspects of your life that are foundational to who you are and what you believe. They provide the lens through which you view life, make decisions, and chart your course. The main benefit of knowing your values is that you will gain tremendous clarity and focus, but ultimately you must use that newfound clarity to make consistent decisions and take committed action. The whole point of discovering your values is to improve the results you get in the areas that are truly most important to you.

Values are priorities that tell you how to spend your time, right here, right now. There are two reasons that priorities are important for our lives. The first reason is that time is our most limited resource. Time does not renew itself; once a day goes by, it's gone forever. If we waste that day by investing our time in actions that don't produce the results we want, that loss is permanent. We can earn more money, improve our physical bodies, and repair broken relationships, but we cannot redo yesterday. If we all had infinite time, values and priorities would be irrelevant. But here on Earth, we appear to be mortal with limited life-spans, and if we value our mortal lives, then it's logical that we invest them as best we can.

I recently had the opportunity to partner with a CEO of a privately held sales, service, and direct distribution company in the creation of the organization's values. The company had a clear culture of God-centered principles, but the specific values had not been clarified. As is the case with most privately held companies, the CEO's personality and beliefs had a great impact on the essence of the company. The CEO wanted to formalize and clearly articulate those values that he held to be so important to all members of the organization so they too could understand what living the values on a daily basis meant. Through multiple meetings, individual interviews, and collaborative work, we were able to define the five core values of the company—integrity, excellence, unity, discipline, and commitment—and develop narratives to bring the values to life. The experience of clarifying these values was invaluable for the CEO and for all team members, as they now share a common understanding.

Life Purpose Statement

The two most important days in your life are the day you are born and the day you find out why.
Mark Twain

As you continue to refine the picture of your life to RESET yourself

and your direction, keep in mind that the purpose statement should be a five- to seven-word statement that encapsulates your mission, vision, and values in a succinct yet highly compelling, emotional, and meaningful phrase. That one phrase should clearly articulate your core values. The life purpose statement should be broad enough to cover multiple areas of life but narrow enough to give you a clear focus for your life and a reason for living.

My purpose statement was developed over several months of self-reflection and prayer. Now that it is complete, it provides a clear lens through which all that I do in life is evaluated. My life purpose statement is the following: "Changing lives...growing leaders: I bring hope, healing, and inspiration to everyone I meet as I lead on the journey for change, growth, and success!"

When I read those words, I experience a sense of deep emotion as I understand that this brief statement is the essence of who I am and why I am here to live my life. This life purpose statement addresses all roles that I will fulfill in my brief time on this Earth. As a husband and father, my purpose is to create an environment where my family — my children in particular — can grow, learn, be encouraged, and realize all of the success that they were created to achieve. As an executive and organizational consulting psychologist, my focus is clearly on working with individuals and organizations to help them continually transform to meet the increasing challenges of an ever-demanding marketplace, grow to unleash their full potential, and achieve the success for which they are striving. Since I am a success coach for CEOs and executives, my purpose statement is the foundation for every conversation that I engage in. In those situations, it is not my picture of "change, growth, and success" that is being explored, but rather my role as a collaborative sojourner that reveals for my clients these personal aspects of their life's journey.

Ultimately, the life purpose statement requires the integration of the mission, vision, and values aspects of self into one clear and riveting statement that is the culmination of all you are and that provides a continual filter for all you do.

Beginning the Journey to Clarifying Purpose:
Identifying Your Mission, Vision, Values, and Life Purpose

To begin the thought process of clarifying your purpose, take the next seven days to answer the following questions. These questions, when answered with the appropriate degree of thought and introspection, may be challenging. I also recommend that during this experience you take the opportunity to journal about what you are thinking, feeling, and experiencing.

This important step will help to provide insight into yourself and can be used in the next section on identifying your passion and understanding your personal "why?"

What will be the center of your life?
What will be the contribution of your life?
What do you want to be known for?
How do you define success?
What are you doing when you realize the greatest personal satisfaction and fulfillment?
What do you most enjoy doing in your professional life?
What do you most enjoy doing in your personal life?
What are your strengths?
What values do you hold most dear? (Feel free to peruse the "Values Identification" section at the back of this book for a list of values as you are identifying those that have the greatest personal meaning for you.)
How do you define those values?
Answering the above questions can start you on the path of identifying and clarifying your purpose.

Passion

Passion is a critical step in success. Your desire determines your destiny. The stronger your fire, the greater the desire—and the greater the potential.

Dr. John Maxwell, author of "The 21 Irrefutable Laws of Leadership"

The second dimension in creating a path toward success is passion. There are multiple definitions of passion, according to *Merriam-Webster*. The one that most closely matches what passion means in the context of RESET is "the emotions as distinguished from reason; intense, driving, or overmastering feeling or conviction; an object of desire or deep interest."[6] With this in mind, it is clear that inherent in passion is the aspect of emotion, which is the driving force of action. Ultimately, passion is about answering the question, "What is my 'why?'"

In exploring this dimension of direction, we will refer back to Newtonian physics, which in actuality have a strong correlation to human behavior. Newton's First Law states, "An object at rest tends to stay at rest."[7] This law applies brilliantly to our behavior as well. As much as we may like to say that we enjoy change, the reality is that often change brings about feelings of anxiety and fear. As a result, it is easier to remain where we are than to take a risk for change. Thus, objects at rest tend to stay at rest.

When living a life of intentional progress, passion is the fuel and energy needed to move you from where you are to where you need to be to fulfill your purpose and achieve success. Passion turbo-charges your actions, allowing you to break free from the chains that would seek to hold you where you are. Unleashing the power of

125

passion requires you to understand the reason that you are pursuing purpose and success; it is answering your "why?"

Why do you get out of bed on those ice-cold mornings in the dead of winter to head off to work? Why do you make it a point to attend all of your children's sporting events, even though you are tired or have other things that you would rather be doing at that point in time? Why, regardless of the challenges of life, do you remain committed to your spouse after fifteen years of marriage? Why do you wake up early each day to spend time in the gym or opt for the turkey burger instead of the more fattening beef option? Why, after being out of school for ten years, do you decide it is time to return to finish your degree or to start a new one? Why do you devote 10 percent of your salary to give to charity? Why do you have a desire to invest in the lives of others, to achieve financial independence, to live a life of balance, to be all you were created to be, and to leave a legacy? Finding your unique answer to the question of "why?" provides the fuel to move forward with pursuing your purpose.

My "why?" has always been clear to me, and I believe it actually began when my parents gave me my name. "Jason" in Greek means "healer." When I first became aware of the etiology of my name at around the age of six, I remember having a desire to see hope and healing in others I had been in contact with. It didn't seem at that time to be a conscious decision to bring healing to others. In reality, at that early season of my life, I knew little about the different areas in which healing could be offered. Rather, it was more of an outpouring of who I was than what I did. I was able to leverage this "why?" in multiple ways throughout my career as a human resource professional. And today, as an entrepreneur, executive, organizational consulting psychologist, professor, trusted advisor to CEOs and executives, author, professional speaker, husband, father, and friend, I enjoy having so many opportunities to bring personal and professional change, growth, success, and healing to people. My passion is fueled when I see people and organizations grow, reach their greatest potential, and become more than they could have ever imagined.

Purpose and passion are inextricably linked. Having one without the other is unproductive and will stand as a barrier to achieving success. Once clarity of purpose is achieved, passion provides the motivation to forge ahead through obstacles that would stand in the way of achieving that purpose. You must have a clear understanding—not only mentally, but, more importantly, emotionally—of the reason that you are on your path. As your perceived purpose moves closer to your innate purpose, your passion will increase. Therefore, there must be a burning sense of urgency for the achievement of purpose. It is this desire that is the motivation behind your actions and behaviors, which in turn result in the realization of success.

Beginning the Journey to Building and Unleashing Your Passion

Building and unleashing your passion begins with an understanding of where your emotional energy comes from. Answer the following questions:

1. What is your "why"?

2. What makes your heart beat fast?

3. Where do you gain your energy?

4. What is your greatest motivator?

As you understand your purpose and passion and see how these two dimensions work together to provide a foundation of direction and momentum, you will be able to move to the next dimension of direction and establish plans for moving forward on your life RESET.

Planning

If you fail to plan, you plan to fail.
Harvey MacKay, author of "Swim With the Sharks Without Being Eaten Alive"

The third dimension of creating a clear direction is that of planning. Once purpose is clarified and passion is unleashed, it is important to develop a map for achieving that purpose. Establishing the course is much like using a GPS. When you enter your car and turn on the GPS unit, the first question asked of you is, "What is the final destination you wish to achieve?" Once you begin your journey, the GPS clearly communicates turn-by-turn directions that allow you to arrive, hopefully safely and in the time anticipated. Two important aspects, therefore, are a having a clear understanding of that end goal and identifying what specific steps or actions you must take to get you there.

As a young boy, I learned the importance of planning for the weekly treat of Saturday morning cartoons. Unlike today, when entertainment for children can be found on no less than fifteen cable and satellite TV channels twenty-four hours a day, watching cartoons back then was reserved for one day a week. Saturday morning cartoons were a thrill that I looked forward to all week long. My favorite was *Super Friends,* and I waited with eager anticipation for 7:00 a.m. to arrive each Saturday. I would position myself in front of the television for sixty minutes of being transported to the Hall of Justice and of sharing in the adventures of Superman, Wonder Woman, Aquaman, Batman and Robin, and the Wonder Twins, Zan and Janya.

I would set my alarm on Friday night for 6:30 a.m. before going to sleep. I knew that this would give me enough time to fully wake

129

up, prepare my bowl of cereal, and assume my position. Looking back today as an adult, I laugh at myself as I consider the planning that was devoted to this weekly ritual. However, to a little boy with a passion for this television show, the commitment to planning to ensure that everything was just right was a discipline that was well worth it.

Develop a Vivid Picture of the End Result

As previously mentioned, it is important to enter the journey to success with the end in mind. This involves having a crystal-clear picture of what success looks like firmly placed in your mind. Suppose, for example, that you have identified your purpose as being a devoted and loving parent who cares deeply for and is actively involved in your children's lives. Your passion is fueled by a deep love for your family and awareness that children are a gift from God and that they are entrusted to you for their care, nurturing, instruction, and growth. With this purpose and passion clearly articulated, you can then move forward with planning. Journey with me as we create that vivid picture in our minds.

You are sitting outside during a cool fall morning at the soccer field, watching and cheering as your six-year-old son is kicking the ball down the field for another goal. The dew is still on the ground, and the fall colors in the leaves are just starting to change. The other parents around are cheering for their children as well, and you suddenly jump from your seat as your "soccer champion" makes that final last push to score the winning point for the team. The crowd goes wild, and as he runs to your arms for a big hug, you realize that you have not only achieved your purpose of being actively involved in your child's life by making this time a priority, but have also fueled your passion by experiencing the joy that comes from caring deeply for your son and being there to nurture and celebrate his victories.

It is with this level of detail that you should enter the process of establishing the results that you wish to achieve. Although this example focused on devoting time to the family, the same approach can be taken for any area of life, personal or professional. Interestingly, you can also use this approach as you strive to achieve a greater sense of life balance. Vivid mental imagery of the future you wish to create is the foundation for developing a compelling and engaging plan.

Perform a Gap Analysis

Once the end result is established, the next step in the planning dimension is to perform a gap analysis. In the gap analysis, you identify what needs to change in order to achieve the end result. Suppose you have an end result goal of having a networking lunch with one new acquaintance per week. Currently, you have a networking lunch about one time per month, so the gap would require you to schedule three additional networking lunches per month.

A gap analysis can be a powerful tool to use in planning because it provides the opportunity to view where you are currently and where you want to go. It enables you to celebrate the successes of what you have achieved and to maintain an awareness of opportunities for the future.

Establish Goals

A dream is just a dream. A goal is a dream with a plan and a deadline.
Harvey MacKay, New York Times Bestselling author

-

While there are many approaches to establishing goals, one that is used widely in personal and professional settings and is most likely already familiar to you is the SMARTS goal structure. It is critical that you find the balance between a goal that is too easy and a goal that is impossible to achieve. The best goal is one that is difficult, allowing you the opportunity to stretch and grow, yet attainable.

SMARTS goals help to create a consistent structure that you can use to develop goals and hold yourself accountable to achieving results. The acronym SMARTS stands for Specific, Measurable, Action-oriented, Reasonable, Time-bound, and Stretch.

The "**specific**" part of the acronym focuses on the need to establish a clear expectation of what will be done or accomplished. It is important to provide enough detail so that there is no doubt in your mind about what exactly should be occurring when the goal is achieved.

The "**measurable**" part of the acronym involves deciding how results will be measured. You want to ensure that progress toward the accomplishment of a goal can be evaluated. Questions such as "How much?," "How many?," and "How will I know when it is accomplished?" should be answered when establishing the measurable aspects of goals.

Action-oriented goals are those that use action words (i.e. attend, meet, schedule) to describe what should be occurring, rather than passive actions (i.e. hope, consider, think about). This approach will allow you to clearly describe what should be happening and what you will be doing differently.

The "**realistic**" aspect refers to the fact that you should be able to successfully complete the goal as it is written. You need to have a personal commitment from yourself and accountability from others to achieve goals that have been established.

The "**time-bound**" aspect refers to the deadline by which the goal should be completed. It is important to set realistic time frames for completing the goal. This will help you stay on track and give you a definite finish line for which to strive.

Stretch goals are those that challenge you to become even better. It is critical that you find the balance between a goal that is too easy and the goal that is impossible to achieve. The best goal is the one that is difficult but attainable.

Using the example of scheduling a networking lunch once a week, the following is a SMARTS model that could be established for the attainment of this goal.

Goal	"Participate in one networking lunch with a new acquaintance per week."
Specific	• I will participate in one networking lunch per week with a new acquaintance. • I will make four calls per week to Vice President and above level professionals in the local business community, introduce myself, and invite them to lunch with the intent of getting to know them better.
Measurable	• One networking lunch per week • Four networking invitation calls per week to Vice President and above level professionals
Action-oriented	• I will participate in one networking lunch per week. • I will make four cold networking calls per week.
Realistic	• By using existing networks, the Book of Lists from my local area, resources from the Chamber of Commerce, and local professional and community organizations as referral sources, I believe this is attainable. • My schedule allows me to schedule one networking lunch per week without compromise. • My current financial situation will allow me to pay for lunch for myself and a guest once per week.
Time-bound	• Beginning January 1 and ending on December 31. During this time, I will have met 52 executives who were not originally part of my network in the local market.
Stretch	• Going from one lunch to four lunches per month is a stretch. I will be challenged to maintain momentum and work through scheduling challenges that naturally accompany individuals at this level of organizations. However, I do believe that although a stretch, it is attainable.

Having a clear plan will bring you the greatest results. You may have experienced seasons when you set goals and achieved all that you wanted to accomplish. However, you also may have set goals and not been as successful as you would have liked. Although this may seem burdensome at first, holding to the process and creating a sense of accountability will increase the probability of success. One important reminder is to keep the number of goals that you establish at a manageable level. High achievers often create goals in multiple areas of life, only to find that it is impossible to achieve them all. Discouragement sets in, and a feeling of failure can emerge. I recommend no more than three to five goals at any given time. This allows you the opportunity to focus on those goals, achieve the results you desire, and ultimately establish habits that will continue long after the time-bound season of the goals are complete.

The achievement of one goal should be the starting point of another.
Alexander Graham Bell, inventor

Surround Yourself with the Right People

Surround yourself with the dreamers and the doers, the believers and the thinkers, but most of all, surround yourself with those who see the greatness within you, even when you don't see it yourself.
Edmund Lee, author, entrepreneur, speaker

We are on our own unique journey in life but are not alone. On a daily basis we are surrounded by others who impact our lives in various ways. Sometimes the relationships we have are uplifting, encouraging, and motivating. Other times the relationships can be draining, demoralizing, and even destructive. Although there may be some exceptions, in general we have the ability to make choices regarding the people we associate with and the type of relationship we share with them. Some of the choices may be difficult, but we do have choices to make. This is a particularly difficult aspect of planning.

In my coaching work, I had a particular CEO client who was struggling with maintaining focus on his purpose and staying committed to the goals he had established. As we worked together, we began to explore the key individuals and relationships in his life. He openly shared that he had surrounded himself with lifelong "friends" who really had little knowledge of the issues he was facing on a daily basis as the leader of a corporation. While he enjoyed spending time with those friends, he felt quite alone, as he really could not discuss the daily challenges he was facing due to a lack of common frame of reference. Ultimately he made the decision to expand his network of friends to include other CEOs who could empathize with the current situations he was facing and provide collaborative support. He still enjoyed time with his longtime friends but was able to release them from the expectation of being able to provide encouragement in the areas of corporate leadership and just enjoy time with them as buddies.

It is suggested that we assume the characteristics of the six people we associate with the most. If this is the case, the importance of being thoughtful about those who you choose to spend your time with cannot be underestimated. Think about the people who are closest to you.

- What characteristics do they demonstrate?
- Are they generally optimistic, encouraging, motivating, and joyful?
- Are they living a life of success and achieving goals that they have established for themselves?
- Do they have dreams that they can clearly articulate and have definite plans to achieve those dreams?

By carefully selecting our partners, mentors, coaches, and friends, we can ensure that we are surrounding ourselves with people who will provide what we need to accomplish our plans and goals.

Beginning the Journey to Establishing a Plan

To begin establishing your plan, answer the following questions:

1. With your purpose in mind, what would you be doing differently that would let you know that you are living your purpose?

2. What do you need to begin doing differently today that will allow you to live your purpose?

3. With your life balance assessments in mind, what aspects do you need to focus on developing? What are one or two things that you can do differently in those areas that would be better for you?

4. With the end result in mind, what would you want to be saying, doing, thinking, and feeling...

    a. Six months from now?

    b. One year from now?

    c. Three years from now?

    d. Five years from now?

    e. Ten years from now?

5. What do you need to do differently today to allow you to achieve that six-month, one-, three-, five-, and ten-year picture?

6. List your six closest friends. List the top three characteristics of each of these individuals. How do those characteristics align with who you are and where you are going?

7. List your six closest work colleagues. List the top three characteristics of each of these individuals. How do those characteristics align with who you are and where you are going?

8. What are the names of the individuals in your life you should be spending more time with because they would be a positive influence on you?

9. What are the names of the individuals in your life you should be spending less time with because they are detracting from you being able to accomplish your goals?

10. What are the names of five individuals you currently do not have a relationship with but who would be valuable to you in providing support in helping you to achieve your goals?

With the answers to these questions, you can begin to develop SMARTS goals and establish clear plans for achieving your end result. You will also be making more strategic decisions about the people with whom you interact and will be selecting those individuals who will encourage, support, and provide insight to you based on their experience. Remember that as you continue on your journey, obstacles will arise. It is during these times of challenge that persistence will be needed more than ever. That is what the next dimension is all about.

Persistence

There is a difference between interest and commitment. When you are interested in doing something, you do it when it is convenient. When you are committed to something, you accept no excuses.
Ken Blanchard, author of "The One Minute Manager"

As with any journey, there often come times when challenges will arise that could stand in your way of achieving the end goal. It is during such times that you have a choice to either forge ahead or turn back. At that critical crossroad, you need to make the all-important decision to retreat to the comfort of the familiar or to "burn the ships."

The phrase "burn the ships" comes from a historic conquest. In 1519, Spanish Conquistador Hernando Cortez landed in Mexico on the shores of the Yucatan with only one objective: to seize the great treasures hoarded by the Aztecs. Cortez was committed to his mission, and his quest for riches is legendary.

For Cortez, the answer was easy. Total commitment was the only option. Although Cortez was resolute, his men were not as convinced. To gain their "buy-in," he took away the option of failure. The only two options that were available to them were to fight to achieve victory or die. When Cortez arrived on the shores of the Yucatan with his men, he rallied them for one final pep talk before leading them into battle and uttering these three words: "Burn the ships."

Amazingly, the men conquered the Aztecs and succeeded in something that others had been unsuccessfully trying to do for six centuries. Why did they win? They had no escape. They had no choice. It was succeed or die. Their ships had been burned. They had no way to get back. Their backs were to the wall.

To really succeed you must have an attitude much like that of Cortez and his men. Cortez and his men did not have a crutch or fallback position. You must persist through all obstacles with the intent of achieving your goal—no questions asked.

Although you may not be in a position that requires such radical action, there are some important steps that you can take as you are moving through your journey that will help you persevere and achieve success.

Constantly Adapt

The first key point to recognize is that with any goal, situations and conditions change. You must continually evaluate the situation and make modifications as needed so that you are able to stay on track. Consider, for example, an airline flight from Los Angeles to New York. The distance between these two locations is approximately 2,400 miles. During the flight, pilots are constantly making minor modifications as a result of wind, atmospheric changes, flight pattern redirections, etc., to ensure that the plane and all its passengers arrive safely at the intended destination. Suppose a pilot set a course that was off by only five degrees; that does not seem like much, but over the course of the trip, it would result in the final landing being approximately two hundred miles off course! By continually adapting to the changing conditions, you are able to stay on course and reach your destination.

Identify and Overcome Obstacles

Great works are performed not by strength, but persistence.
Dr. Samuel Johnson, British author and linguist

The next critical aspect to persistence is to identify and overcome obstacles. In reality, there is no way for us to know every challenge we may face during the pursuit of our goals. We can, however, devote time to evaluating our situation, identifying obstacles, and developing approaches to avoid them. Constant awareness of potential risks brings us to the point of being the captains of our destiny, rather than just passengers.

Internal Motivation (IM)

Success is a little like wrestling a gorilla. You don't quit when you are tired—you quit when the gorilla is tired.
Robert Strauss, "Sports Illustrated" writer

The third behavior that increases persistence is internal motivation, or IM. This is the fortitude that you maintain inside that keeps you moving in the direction of the end result that you are seeking. IM and discipline prevents you from eating that piece of chocolate cake when you have a goal of losing ten pounds in the next four weeks before your class reunion. It is what gets you out of bed every morning to work out so you have a greater probability of enjoying a healthier and more active life in your later years. It is that internal force that keeps you going when all else tells you to stop.

This concept of internal motivation was never as real to me as it was when I faced the incredibly daunting experience of writing the dissertation for my doctor of philosophy degree. There came a moment when I reached a point of exhaustion and frustration that resulted in me being "stuck." I literally had ten boxes of research that I needed to integrate into a literature review. I remember sitting in my office day after day, looking at the boxes of research and thinking that it was an insurmountable mountain of information that I needed to synthesize in order to move forward with my final doctoral work. I would rationalize my delay by turning my attention to other activities that I convinced myself were more important. Thus, a pattern of procrastination and rationalization had taken hold, and while I knew that I needed to redirect my internal motivation to tackle this goal, making the change was becoming increasingly difficult.

After approximately two months of looking at the research and making excuses as to why I could not start, I became so disgusted with myself and my inability to move forward that I closed the doors to my office and just began writing. The road to change often begins with just one—often painful—first step. I wrote for almost two days straight, taking time to break only for a quick meal and to get four hours of sleep. The end result was a complete literature review and a feeling of success for being able to move forward with my research. In this case, my personal momentum had stalled and I had to face the task of "resetting" my engine so that I could accomplish what needed to be done. Be aware of the risk of stopping, and keep your motivation at a level that will allow you to continue to realize progress, regardless of the amount, on a daily basis.

Developing New Habits

Setting and achieving your goals will involve a change in behavior and the formation of new habits. You are creating a structure that will force you to focus on new actions which, when repeated over time, will become part of your daily life. Taking the first step in the formation of a new habit can be difficult. It requires a mental commitment that does not accept any alternative other than to move forward with the behaviors that will ultimately form the habit that is desired.

Habits are not easy to form; doing so takes discipline and diligence. With focus and perseverance, however, turning certain behaviors into habits will become much easier. Then you will be able to move on to developing new habits that will be valuable.

Support and Accountability

No one is an island, and on the journey to success, we all need others who can celebrate with us when we achieve our goals and hold us accountable when we do not. Accountability is about asking the tough questions in a supportive and encouraging way.

I have moved through different seasons of my life when accountability was either more or less prevalent. The establishment of an effective "accountability group" involves a great deal of thought, and several factors are essential. First, while not all members of the group need to share the same experiences, there must be a common thread of interest and desire among the members that can be a foundation for mutual accountability. A group that is unequally yoked could lead to frustration for the members and a lack of shared direction.

Second, there must be a commitment between all participants to invest in the lives of others. Each individual demonstrates this by setting time aside to connect, support, and encourage others. Meeting times should be preserved as an essential aspect of the week and protected to the greatest extent possible.

Third, the group should work together to establish a set of ground rules that all members will share. Ideas such as open discussion, confidentiality, mutual respect, a desire to understand each other fully, and a commitment to meeting on a regular basis are often included in the values of accountability groups.

I have a group of men who I meet with on a weekly basis. During this time, we share our goals and we ask what I call the "3 Big Questions" of each other:

- What is working well?
- What is not working well?
- What do you need to do differently that would be better for you?

These three questions allow us to share briefly as we reflect on the week, look ahead, and consider what may need to change for us to stay or get back on track. I have also found that I do not want to disappoint these gentlemen, so when I face obstacles, I have an external motivation of "I do not want to have to report that I failed," which helps me to persevere.

Honesty, transparency, and trust are foundational behaviors that are essential for healthy and successful accountability groups. The value of accountability is fully realized when all participants are able to experience the freedom to share openly, encourage greatly, and confront appropriately in a nonjudgmental way.

Beginning the Journey to Maintaining Persistence

Persistence in any endeavor is critical. By answering the following questions, you will be able to create a support structure that you can leverage when you face times of opposition, either externally or internally, on your journey to success.

1. Who are three individuals with whom you can share your plans and goals and who will help to hold you accountable?

2. What are some times when you were able to overcome obstacles? What specifically did you do? What did you learn that you could apply in the future?

3. What can you use as your IM to ensure that you stay on track

toward the accomplishment of your goals?

4. What consistent and planned time do you need to set aside for personal reflection to identify those needed course corrections? When will you do that? Where will you go to be able to get away by yourself for the time of reflection?

As you persist on your journey, you will no doubt reach a time when you achieve the goals that you established. At that point, it is important to take time to celebrate your successes and express gratitude. This is the focus of the fifth and final dimension of life direction.

Gratitude

To be great, be grateful.
Jim Rohn, author and motivational speaker

The road to success is not easy. You will need to make sacrifices, work hard, and give of yourself. But the destination is worth all of the effort you give, not only for yourself, but also for those you love. Taking time to celebrate is essential as you reflect on what you achieved.

As previously mentioned, I have kept a journal for many years. My father introduced me to this when I entered my undergraduate studies at Purdue University. I remember him encouraging me to write something every day about what happened. It did not have to be earth-shattering; it just had to be something. Although this was a challenge at first, it quickly became a habit. Now, as I have the opportunity to read back through those four journals for the four years I attended that university, I am able to see the strengths I had at the time that allowed me to succeed, but also recognize how I have grown since.

Today, I have developed my journaling into two forms. I still maintain written journals in which I capture quotes that are particularly impactful for me, inspirational messages, thoughts that I have throughout the day, and my goals, plans, and dreams for the future. I also have an audio journal that I transfer to compact disc. My goal is to create a library that I plan to give to my children that will have a record of my thoughts, feelings, and messages to them that are intended to provide them inspiration and encouragement in the future. For now, these are private writings and recordings that allow me the opportunity to express in different forms those things that are so meaningful for me. In the future, they will be part of the legacy and history of my life—a record of my journey—that will be shared with those I loved the most in my life.

There are many different ways to journal, and you may have an approach that you already use. Regardless of the medium, the most important part is to "just do it!" You will never regret the time you spend on this important practice and habit. It will make a significant difference as you give thanks for the successes you achieve.

A second aspect of gratitude is taking time to reflect. Often we are so caught up in the busyness of life that we neglect the need to get away by ourselves and take time to reflect, meditate, and offer thanks for all the blessings in our lives. In 2011, I began a biannual practice of visiting the Abbey at Gethsemani in Trappist, Kentucky. During this three-day retreat at the monastery, I have the opportunity to rid myself of many of the distractions of my busy life (including conversation with others) and focus solely on reflecting on the past, recalibrating my goals to align with my innate purpose, and celebrating anticipated success in the future. It is truly a high-water mark for me and is a vivid reminder of the importance of periodically and decisively taking myself to a place of quiet and solitude where I can listen, reflect, and renew and ensure that all that I am doing, thinking, feeling, and believing is aligned with my highest purpose and ultimate success.

Third, there may also be times when a formal celebration is in order. When I completed my doctor of philosophy degree just before my fortieth birthday, my bride, Darla, orchestrated a wonderful time of celebration, and my friends, colleagues, and family were invited to share their sentiments of congratulations. That was a special time, and although I typically am not someone who has a high need to be in the spotlight, seeing those who provided support, encouragement, and prayer during my journey toward achieving such a monumental accomplishment share in the celebration with me was truly priceless and is the foundation of many great memories today. I encourage you to take the opportunity to formally celebrate your successes. Enjoy your time in the spotlight; you deserve it!

A fourth aspect of gratitude is sharing your appreciation with others. On your journey to success, there will be individuals who provide support, encouragement, or even direct assistance. Family, friends, personal and professional supporters, business partners, and many others will play important roles in your life. Taking an opportunity to reach out personally to those who helped and encouraged you is a great way to encapsulate and live out the spirit of gratitude. All too often opportunities are missed to tell those closest to us how much they truly mean to us. Making a dedicated effort to give thanks in a meaningful, heartfelt way will bring great joy and let those who care so much about you know that you are truly grateful for their place in your life.

Beginning the Journey to Expressing Gratitude and Celebrating Your Successes

Gratitude is an essential part of success. It brings closure to the current process and enables you to celebrate what has happened and begin to transition to the next season of success. The following questions will help you ensure that you are creating an environment in which you can celebrate your success with full gratitude.

1. What will you do to journal or capture the daily/weekly/monthly accomplishments that you achieve?

2. Where can you go to get away and reflect?

3. How often can you and should you get away to reflect?

4. Who do you need to include in your time of celebration? Your spouse? Your parents? Your children?

5. What can you do to formally celebrate your successes?

6. Who do you need to contact to tell them what they have done for you and how much you appreciate them?

Life Direction: Conclusion

The five dimensions of life direction provide the framework for you to move toward realizing your greatest success. By clearly understanding your purpose and the source of your passion, you can create the foundational conditions for realizing your potential. As you establish plans that align with your purpose, you develop the habits that will continue into the future and allow you to live your purpose in even bigger ways. When obstacles arise, persistence and discipline in remaining committed to your purpose and goals are essential. But as you overcome the challenges that would seek to thwart your progress, you are able to celebrate with those who have supported, encouraged, and walked with you on your journey.

It is important to remember that success is not a destination, but rather a continual process. Once one season is complete, another begins. You have the privilege and responsibility to continually seek to live out your greatest potential, to realize your purpose, and, through planning and persistence, to achieve the pinnacle of success that only you were created to achieve.

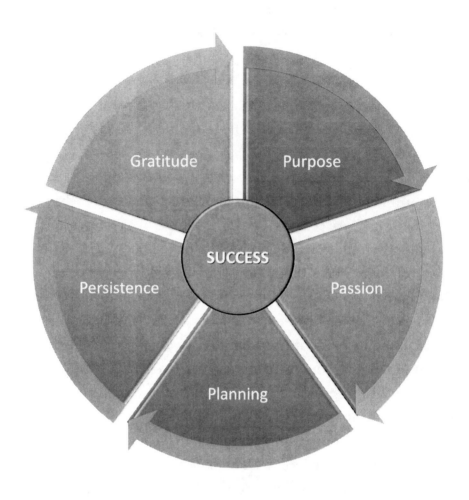

Five Dimensions of Direction –
P^{4}G Model

Unleashing Your Success

Success is not measured by what you do compared to others; it is measured by what you do with the ability God gave you.
Zig Ziglar, author, salesman, and motivational speaker

Achieving a successful RESET, which entails being able to integrate the aspects of balance and direction, begins with having a clear picture of your desired result and ultimate success. Therefore, just as you have a life purpose statement, it is also important to have a life success statement. This is a statement that clearly articulates what success ultimately looks like for you. Your life success statement should be resolute yet provide for flexibility of different roads that can be taken to attain that success. The life success statement provides a concise and clear depiction of what success is in your life. It vividly answers the question, "What will be happening that will lead me to know that I am living a life of success?" This success statement can take many forms and directions but is grounded in the alignment of mission, vision, values, and results. It should be sufficiently clear so as to leave little doubt as to when success has been achieved.

My life success statement brings together the tangible goals of creating a successful business, living out my core values, and focusing on individual change, growth, and success. It is a continual reminder to me of what success looks like and enables me to make decisions that bring me one step closer to achieving success. Based on my research, this is a concept unique to The RESET Model. I believe, however, that this is essential, as it allows individuals to gain clarity regarding the path for their future and ensures an alignment between purpose and action.

There are several aspects to consider in developing your path to success and your life success statement.

Resources for Success

You will first begin the process of answering the question, "What resources are available to help me obtain my vision of success?" These resources will be either intrinsic (inside of you) or extrinsic (outside of you). Your unique talents and abilities are a resource you will leverage. Your personality, thinking style, behavioral traits, and core interests are just a few examples of things that provide the foundation for the innate resources that are available to you. By having a firm understanding of self, you are in the best position possible to leverage those aspects of who you are that can aid in the attainment of your dreams and to minimize those areas that could be roadblocks to your success. In addition, external factors may also serve as catalysts for moving you in the right direction. These include:

- The support of family, friends, and colleagues
- An investment in personal improvement and education
- Making great decisions for physical health
- Surrounding yourself with a strong social support system
- Making prudent financial decisions that enable you to enjoy your desired standard of living and to give back to others
- The actions that you take daily to maintain a positive mental attitude
- Selecting a career path that is fulfilling and motivating and that allows you to live your life purpose and achieve your statement of success

There are many tools available that can help provide insight into your areas of strength and identify resources that can be used to achieve success. I am a strong advocate for the use of assessments as a starting point for understanding yourself. Instruments such as the Myers Briggs Type Indicator, StrengthsFinder, Strong Interest Inventory, DiSC Personality Profile, and Profiles XT, when administered and interpreted by a trained professional, can unlock amazing personal insight. In addition, the Life Balance Assessments included in this book can be a great foundation for the exploration of extrinsic factors that could be either motivating (those that propel you forward) or restraining (those that hold you back) forces.

Breaking Through the Fear of Success

Next, it is important to recognize and eliminate those things that would serve to stand in your way of accomplishing your full measure of success. Often the greatest barrier to your success is your own fear. Fear is a seductive and powerful influence in our lives. There are many areas of life that can bring feelings of fear, including:

- Fear of failure
- Fear of success
- Fear of conflict
- Fear of losing what we have
- Fear of not correctly discerning and identifying our purpose and passion
- Fear of being called to do something outside our comfort zone
- Fear of the thoughts, perceptions, or impressions of others
- Fear of not being a "real man" or "real woman"
- Fear of losing "control"
- Fear of not accomplishing success

Often these feelings of fear can be so strong that we decide it is better not to try than to risk the potential pain that could come from reaching for the prize. Fear is the destroyer of fully realizing our greatest potential and ultimate success.

To break through the barriers created by fear, it is important to take time to personally explore how fear has taken hold of you and how you have persevered through fear in the past to achieve your dreams. Consider your answers to the following four questions.

1. What fears do you have that would stand in your way of moving forward to achieve success?

2. Think about a time in the past when you overcame your fear and took a risk. What was that like for you? What was the result?

3. What strengths do you have that you can use to overcome your fears?

4. What are some potential missed opportunities that will result if you fall victim to your fears?

Image of Success

Finally, you need to have a vivid image of what life success will look like when achieved. It is important to have a specific, measurable, and time-bound picture of success. It is through this clear vision that success moves from the subconscious world of dreams to the conscious world of achievement.

In clarifying your statement of success and developing your vibrant image, explore answers to the following questions:

1. What will you be doing when you achieve success?

2. What will you be thinking when you achieve success?

3. What will you be feeling when you achieve success?

4. What will others be saying about you?

5. What will you have acquired?

6. What will you have created?

7. What will you have given?

8. Who will be with you?

9. Who will be sitting in the grandstand, cheering you on?

By answering these questions, you will begin to infuse the future success into you today. The greater your ability to experience your success of tomorrow in the now, the faster you will act to achieve your individual and unique success in life. Meditate daily, weekly, monthly, and yearly on this vision, and maintain in the forefront of your thoughts your purpose and picture of success.

Final Thoughts

We come this way but once. We can either tiptoe through life and hope that we get to death without being too badly bruised or we can live a full, complete life achieving our goals and realizing our wildest dreams
Bob Proctor, author of "You Were Born Rich"

To accomplish great things, we must not only act, but also dream, not only plan, but also believe.
Anatole France, French poet, journalist, and novelist

The desire for life success is innate and woven into of the fabric of each of us. However, this innate desire is often hidden under layers of uncertainty, fear, and doubt. I am continually motivated and challenged by the thoughts of Marianne Williamson, who wrote:

> Our deepest fear is not that we are inadequate. Our deepest fear is that we are powerful beyond measure. It is our light, not our darkness, that most frightens us. We ask ourselves, who am I to be brilliant, gorgeous, talented, and fabulous? Actually, who are you not be? Your playing small doesn't serve the world. There's nothing enlightened about shrinking so that other people won't feel insecure around you. We are all meant to shine as children do. We are born to make manifest the glory of our highest potential that is within us. It's not just in some of us, it's in everyone. And as we let our own light shine, we unconsciously give other people permission to do the same. As we are liberated from our own fear, our presence automatically liberates us.[1]

You have taken the first steps toward changing the legacy of your life from one of mediocrity to one of extravagant success. The model and concepts that have been presented, however, will mean little without the discipline, commitment, and dedication to move forward with tenacity and a resolute determination to live—each and every day—the concepts of this model so that you can continue to experience even greater success.

It is important to remember that your RESET is a journey, not a destination. You may identify today that you need a Radical RESET and set forward on a course to change. Once you are redirected you will no doubt continue to engage in a Realigning RESET and Refining RESET for the rest of your life. Making RESET a constant part of your life will ensure that you stay on track and in alignment with your purpose. Not doing so will ultimately lead you off course, bringing you out of alignment with your purpose and moving you in a direction that is not in perfect harmony with your purpose. It will not necessarily be a conscious decision to depart, but with a lack of discipline to the basics comes drifting. Just as a sailor needs to continue to set the sail in response to the changing winds, so too do you need to engage in continual RESET, be it Radical, Realigning, or Refining.

We never reach a point where we arrive. There will always be another dream to dream, another goal to achieve, another life to touch, and another legacy to leave. As such, your journey to life success must be continual. You must strive daily to maintain balance in the physical, social, emotional, intellectual, occupational, spiritual, and financial aspects of life to ensure stability. In addition, you must continually move through the P⁴G model by reevaluating your purpose, reenergizing your passion, establishing clear plans, identifying new ways to overcome obstacles, and taking time to express gratitude to yourself and others for the successes achieved.

Do not wish for a better wind. The key is to pursue the wisdom to set a better sail.
Jim Rohn, author and motivational speaker

Through this process of pursuing your purpose, you are becoming what you were created to be. You are establishing the conditions for success, and as you relentlessly pursue your purpose and become the person you were destined to become, you will see that success is waiting. We are all in a constant state of becoming and are either taking steps toward or away from our success. In the end, you own your own success. No one can create it for you. No one can tell you which path to take on your journey. Instruments and tools can be provided, much like the gyroscope, compass, and The RESET Model. But ultimately, you are the captain of your ship. Here's wishing you calm seas, a strong wind, and the wisdom to set a better sail. Sail away!

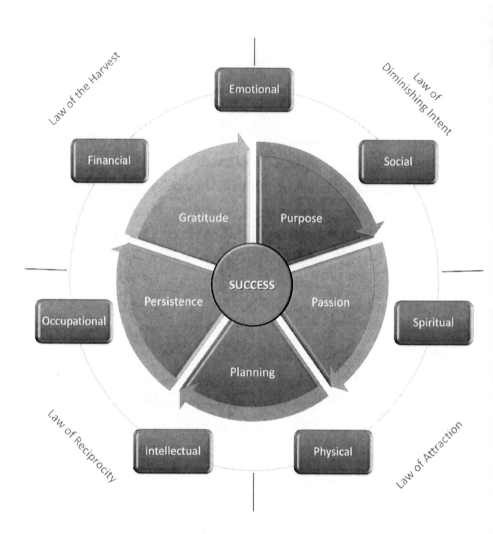

The RESET Model

The End of the Beginning

The journey of a thousand miles begins with a single step.
Lao-tzu, Chinese philosopher

I encourage you to think back to the first reflective exercise in our journey together—the creation of your eulogy. As you will recall, during this experience you were asked to create a story of your life as you went through the early years, the adolescent years, late adolescence, early adulthood, adulthood, late adulthood, and ultimately your passing

When you first held this book in your hand, this may have been a difficult exercise, both mentally and emotionally, to consider. It is my hope and prayer, however, that through the experience we have shared delving into The RESET Model, you can now reconsider the answers to these questions with a clear vision of what your life is and will become.

We started this journey by "beginning at the end." Now you are ready to take the next steps by realizing this is the "end of the beginning." We are at the end of this particular time together, but you are standing at the beginning of your continuing journey to live the full vision of what you dream for your life. You have achieved an understanding of yourself and created the roadmap that will enable you to live your purpose with passion. You have reformatted your life's purpose for tomorrow's world. It is now up to you to devote yourself daily to that purpose. It is important to realize that from time to time you may need a RESET. As a result, I encourage you to keep this model and the concepts close at hand. Do not allow yourself to wander; instead, review the fundamental principles that brought you to this place of realignment that you are celebrating today. The

161

daily disciplines that you have learned and established will be the foundation upon which you will build your life of success. You, like everyone else, are entrusted with 86,400 seconds every day. What you do with those seconds is up to you. Decide now to commit every second you are given to the pursuit of your life dreams and to live your life of purpose with passion!

Afterword

As you reflect on the journey that we have shared, you will no doubt notice that much of the applications, stories, and experiences have been focused on the individual. However, it is important to note that these same concepts and structures apply with equal impact to teams and organizations. After all, in the end, organizations are nothing more than a community of individuals pursuing a common purpose and goal of success.

Many companies today fail to recognize and capitalize on the value that each individual brings. There is a lack of focus or effort to create an environment that allows employees to establish and maintain a sense of balance. In addition, all too often there is not a shared sense of direction. This leads to multiple problems for companies, including a lack of employee engagement, decreased performance, cultural separation, and the ability to meet goals being either greatly slowed or derailed completely.

Companies that create an environment that supports balance for employees and a collaborative sense of direction, where everyone has an opportunity to engage in the strategic direction of the company, will ultimately realize the greatest success. It is not easy, and often it is beneficial for organizations to partner with an external consultant who is experienced in leading and facilitating the path toward change, growth, and transformation. This way, all individuals in the company can participate in building a foundation of balance and direction, rather than being concerned with facilitating the process.

In the end, to the extent that individuals are able to realize and achieve success, organizations are able to achieve the same.

Companies that recognize this path will achieve a competitive advantage in the marketplace as focus is placed on the most valuable resource of any organization—its people. There is a clear connection between individual success and organizational success, and when this dynamic is made a priority and nurtured through systems and processes that are aligned with organizational purposes and goals, amazing results will occur.

Notes

Beginning Your RESET!

1. *Merriam-Webster Online*, s.v. "success," accessed May 30, 2013, http://www.merriam-webster.com/dictionary/success.

Foundational Laws of Success

1. *Merriam-Webster Online*, s.v. "foundation", accessed May 30, 2013, http://www.merriam-webster.com/dictionary/foundation.

2. Stephen Covey, *The 7 Habits of Highly Effective People* (New York: Free Press, 2004).

3. Denis Dyomkin, "Russia Lost Quarter of Grain Crop," Reuters, August 12, 2010, http://www.reuters.com/article/2010/08/12/us-grain-russia-idUSTRE67B2V120100812.

4. James Allen, *As a Man Thinketh* (New York, NY: SoHo Books, 2011).

5. Jack Canfield, *The Success Principles: How to Get from Where You Are to Where You Want to Be* (New York: Collins, 2005).

6. Rhonda Byrne, *The Secret* (New York: Atria Books, 2006).

7. Earl Nightingale, *The Strangest Secret: How to Live the Life You Desire* (Naperville: Simple Truths, LLC, 1952).

Aspects of Balance

1. Patricia Broaderick and Pamela Blewitt, *The Life Span: Human Development for Helping Professionals,* 2nd ed. (Upper Saddle River: Pearson, 2006).

2. Cynthia Chandler, Janice Holden, and Cheryl Kolander, "Counseling for Spiritual Wellness: Theory and Practice," *Journal of Counseling & Development,* vol. 71 (November/December 1992), 168-175.

3. William Hettler, "Wellness: Encouraging a Lifetime Pursuit of Excellence," *Health Values: Achieving High Level Wellness,* vol. 8 (July/August 1984), 13–17.

4. Suzanne Degges-White, Jane Myers, James Adelman, and Denise Pastoor, "Examining Counseling Needs of Headache Patients: An Exploratory Study of Wellness and Perceived Stress," *Journal of Mental Health Counseling,* vol. 25 no. 4 (October 2003), 271–290.

5. John Hattie, Jane Myers, and Thomas Sweeney, "A Factor Structure of Wellness: Theory, Assessment, Analysis, and Practice," *Journal of Counseling & Development,* vol. 82 (Summer 2004), 354–364.

6. David Hermon and Richard Hazler, "Adherence to a Wellness Model and Perceptions of Psychological Well-Being," *Journal of Counseling & Development,* vol. 77 (Summer 1999), 339–343.

7. George Bear, Maureen Manning, and Carol Izard, "Responsible Behavior: The Importance of Social Cognition and Emotion," *School Psychology Quarterly*, vol. 18 no. 2 (Summer 2003), 140–157.

8. "Emotional," National Wellness Institute, accessed June 30,2013, http://c.ymcdn.com/sites/ www.nationalwellness.org/resource/resmgr/docs/ sixdimensionsfactsheet.pdf.

9. Jason Brooks, "The Relationship Between Life Balance and Work Stress in Corporate Executives" (Phd dissertation, Capella University, 2009), http://gradworks. umi.com/33/72/3372244.html.

10. "Social," National Wellness Institute, accessed June 30, 2013, http://c.ymcdn.com/sites/www.nationalwellness. org/resource/resmgr/docs/sixdimensionsfactsheet.pdf.

11. Sharon Brehm, Saul Kassin, and Steven Fein, *Social Psychology*, 6th ed. (Boston: Houghton Mifflin Company, 2005).

12. "Spiritual," National Wellness Institute, accessed June 30, 2013, http://c.ymcdn.com/sites/www.nationalwellness. org/resource/resmgr/docs/sixdimensionsfactsheet.pdf.

13. "Physical," National Wellness Institute, accessed June 30, 2013, http://c.ymcdn.com/sites/www.nationalwellness. org/resource/resmgr/docs/sixdimensionsfactsheet.pdf.

14. Adam Brookover, "What Is the Definition of Nutrition?," HealthGuidance, 2011, http://www. healthguidance.org/entry/9975/1/What-Is-the-Definition-of-Nutrition.html.

15. "14 Keys to a Healthy Diet," Remedy Health Media, LLC, 2011, http://wellnessletter.com/html/fw/fwNut01HealthyDiet.html.

16. "How Much Sleep Do We Really Need?," National Sleep Foundation, 2011, http://www.sleepfoundation.org/article/how-sleep-works/how-much-sleep-do-we-really-need.

17. "Why Is Exercise Important?," Health Discovery Network, 2010, http://www.healthdiscovery.net/articles/exercise_importa.htm.

18. "Intellectual," National Wellness Institute, accessed June 30, 2013, http://c.ymcdn.com/sites/www.nationalwellness.org/resource/resmgr/docs/sixdimensionsfactsheet.pdf.

19. "Occupational," National Wellness Institute, accessed June 30, 2013, http://c.ymcdn.com/sites/www.nationalwellness.org/resource/resmgr/docs/sixdimensionsfactsheet.pdf.

20. Dave Ramsey, The Total Money Makeover (Nashville, TN: Thomas Nelson, 2009).

21. Dave Ramsey, *Financial Peace: Revisited* (New York: Penguin Group, 2003).

22. "Taking the Mystery out of Retirement Planning," United States Department of Labor, 2009, http://www.dol.gov/ebsa/publications/nearretirement.html.

23. "How Much Will You Need for Retirement?," CNN Money, 2011, http://cgi.money.cnn.com/tools/retirementneed/retirementneed_plain.html.

Dimensions of Direction

1. Rick Warren, *The Purpose Driven Life* (Grand Rapids: Zondervan, 2002).

2. "Mission & Values," McDonald's, 2013, http://www.aboutmcdonalds.com/mcd/our_company/mission_and_values.html .

3. "Company Profile," Ken Blanchard Companies, 2013, http://www.kenblanchard.com/About_Ken_Blanchard_Companies/Company_Profile.

4. "Company Overview," Google, 2013, https://www.google.com/intl/en/about/

5. "Investor Relations," The Walt Disney Company, 2013, http://thewaltdisneycompany.com/investors

6. *Merriam-Webster Online*, s.v. "passion," accessed May 30, 2013, http://www.merriam-webster.com/dictionary/passion.

7. "Newton's Laws of Motion," The Physics Classroom, 2012, http://www.physicsclassroom.com/class/newtlaws/u2l1b.cfm.

Final Thoughts

1. Marianne Williamson, *A Return to Love* (New York: Harper Collins, 1992).

Appendices

Assessments of Life Balance
> *Emotional Aspect Assessment*
> *Social Aspect Assessment*
> *Spiritual Aspect Assessment*
> *Physical Aspect Assessment*
> *Intellectual Aspect Assessment*
> *Occupational Aspect Assessment*
> *Financial Aspect Assessment*

Aspects of Balance Scoring Template

Balance Wheel Model

Example of Completed Balance Wheel

Aspects of Balance Action Planning Template

SMARTS Goals Template

Beginning the Journey to Identifying and Clarifying Purpose
> *Your Life Mission Statement*
> *Your Life Vision Statement*
> *Your Life Values*
> *List of Common Values*
> *Your Life Purpose Statement*

Beginning the Journey to Building and Unleashing Your Passion

Beginning the Journey to Establishing a Plan

Beginning the Journey to Maintaining Persistence

Beginning the Journey to Expressing Gratitude and Celebrating Your Successes

Your Success Statement

Assessments of Life Balance

The following assessments provide an opportunity for you to gain awareness into your wellness in each aspect of life balance. You are encouraged to use the assessments to obtain insight into your personal balance and then develop actions plans based on the SMARTS format that is presented in the "Direction" section to provide a greater sense of overall balance.

Emotional Wellness Assessment

The emotional aspect of balance involves recognizing, accepting and taking responsibility for your feelings. Read each statement carefully and respond honestly by using the following scoring:

Strongly Agree	4 Points
Agree	3 Points
Disagree	2 Points
Strongly Disagree	1 Point

	I feel positive about myself and my life.
	I am able to form and maintain strong personal relationships.
	I am able to be the person that I choose to be and accept responsibility for my actions.
	I believe that challenges and change are opportunities for personal growth.
	I believe that I am performing to the best of my ability and that I am living my greatest potential.
	I understand and can adjust to life's ups and down effectively.
	I appropriately cope with stress and make time for activities that provide an opportunity for me to rest, relax, and recharge.
	I am able to recognize and express my feelings effectively.
	I am non-judgmental in my approach to others.
	I love life and enjoy making the most of each day.
	Total for Emotional Wellness Aspect

Score: **32-40 Points** – This aspect is a great strength for you and most likely is a source of satisfaction and stability in your life.

Score: **19-32 Points** – While not an immediate issue, there is opportunity to improve in this area.

Score: **10-18 Points** - This aspect is an issue for you and requires dedicated focus to avoid creating imbalance overall in your life.

Social Wellness Assessment

The social aspect of balance involves developing, nourishing and encouraging satisfying relationships. Read each statement carefully and respond honestly by using the following scoring:

Strongly Agree 4 Points
Agree 3 Points
Disagree 2 Points
Strongly Disagree 1 Point

	I have at least one person in my life who I consider a great confidant and best friend.
	My relationships with my family are positive and uplifting.
	I am able to develop close, personal relationships.
	I am interested in others, including those who have different backgrounds and experiences from me.
	I am involved in activities in my local community where I volunteer and serve others.
	I have an awareness of other's needs and help others when possible.
	I do something for fun and just for myself at least once a week.
	I am able to effectively balance my needs with the needs of others.
	I enjoy spending time with others and am able to develop a personal connection with others.
	I place value on relationships and strive daily to improve relationships with those in my life.
	Total for Social Wellness Aspect

Score: **32-40 Points** – This aspect is a great strength for you and most likely is a source of satisfaction and stability in your life.

Score: **19-32 Points** – While not an immediate issue, there is opportunity to improve in this area.

Score: **10-18 Points** - This aspect is an issue for you and requires dedicated focus to avoid creating imbalance overall in your life.

Spiritual Wellness Assessment

The spiritual aspect of balance involves seeking meaning and purpose in one's life. Read each statement carefully and respond honestly by using the following scoring:

Strongly Agree   4 Points
Agree   3 Points
Disagree   2 Points
Strongly Disagree   1 Point

	I have a clear understanding of the purpose of my life and the reason that I am living.
	The goals and activities that I engage are consistent with my purpose.
	I am comfortable with my spiritual life.
	I live my life in alignment between my values and my daily actions.
	I engage consistently in times of prayer, meditation, or quiet personal reflection.
	When I am feeling overwhelmed or depressed, my spiritual life is a source of direction and inspiration for me.
	I am willing to consider new and different ideas even if they do not make sense to me initially.
	I am optimistic about life and seek to live my life in self-affirming ways.
	I am able to forgive others easily for wrongs that have been committed against me.
	I am able to forgive myself easily for wrongs that I have committed against others.
	Total for Spiritual Wellness Aspect

Score: **32-40 Points** – This aspect is a great strength for you and most likely is a source of satisfaction and stability in your life.

Score: **19-32 Points** – While not an immediate issue, there is opportunity to improve in this area.

Score: **10-18 Points** - This aspect is an issue for you and requires dedicated focus to avoid creating imbalance overall in your life.

Physical Wellness Assessment

The physical aspect of balance involves encouraging regular activities that produce endurance, flexibility and strength. Read each statement carefully and respond honestly by using the following scoring:

Strongly Agree	4 Points
Agree	3 Points
Disagree	2 Points
Strongly Disagree	1 Point

	I engage in vigorous aerobic exercise for 20 to 30 minutes at least three times a week
	I make nutrition a priority and eat fruits, vegetables, and whole grains every day.
	I do not engage in the use of tobacco products.
	I consciously minimize the consumption of cholesterol, dietary fats, and oils.
	I do not engage in the consumption of alcohol or limit myself to no more than one drink per day.
	I get the appropriate amount of sleep for my age and wake in the morning feeling rested and refreshed.
	I make good choices regarding my safety including wearing a seat belt and avoiding texting when driving.
	I am able to effectively manage stress in my life.
	I put a high priority on my health by staying current on medical and dental examinations, immunizations, and visit the doctor if issues arise.
	I maintain an appropriate and consistent (avoiding extremes) weight for my age and body composition.
	Total for Physical Wellness Aspect

Score: **32-40 Points** – This aspect is a great strength for you and most likely is a source of satisfaction and stability in your life.

Score: **19-32 Points** – While not an immediate issue, there is opportunity to improve in this area.

Score: **10-18 Points** - This aspect is an issue for you and requires dedicated focus to avoid creating imbalance overall in your life.

Intellectual Wellness Assessment

The intellectual aspect of balance involves embracing creativity and mental stimulation. Read each statement carefully and respond honestly by using the following scoring:

Strongly Agree 4 Points
Agree 3 Points
Disagree 2 Points
Strongly Disagree 1 Point

	I am interested in learning just for the joy of learning.
	I believe that my education has prepared me for what I would like to accomplish in life.
	I enjoy sharing with others the things that I have learned.
	I am selective in how I spend my time and avoid activities that would be mentally stagnating.
	I am able to analyze, synthesize, and evaluate multiple aspects of a discussion or issue.
	I am interested in the viewpoint of others, even if it is different from my own.
	I am motivated to learn and improve myself.
	I enjoy reading a variety of materials and am consistently spending time in this activity.
	I understand the importance of personal continuous improvement and actively participate in activities that challenge me to grow.
	I seek opportunities to keep informed of current affairs locally, nationally, and internationally.
	Total for Intellectual Wellness Aspect

Score: **32-40 Points** – This aspect is a great strength for you and most likely is a source of satisfaction and stability in your life.

Score: **19-32 Points** – While not an immediate issue, there is opportunity to improve in this area.

Score: **10-18 Points** - This aspect is an issue for you and requires dedicated focus to avoid creating imbalance overall in your life.

Occupational Wellness Assessment

The occupational aspect of balance involves choosing a career/job that is rewarding and enjoyable. Read each statement carefully and respond honestly by using the following scoring:

Strongly Agree   4 Point
Agree   3 Points
Disagree   2 Points
Strongly Disagree   1 Point

	I am happy with the choice I made in my career.
	I enjoy my work and experience fulfillment in what I do.
	The responsibilities I have in my job are consistent with my personal values.
	The rewards that are available in my job are consistent with my personal values.
	I am satisfied with the balance I am able to maintain between my professional and personal time.
	I am content with the degree of autonomy and control that I have in my current occupation.
	The work that I do provides a sense of personal satisfaction and motivation.
	I am satisfied with the growth potential that I have in my job and can see opportunities to develop in the future.
	I believe I am able to make a difference through the work I do.
	Overall, my job contributes to my personal and professional well-being.
	Total for Occupational Wellness Aspect

Score: **32-40 Points** – This aspect is a great strength for you and most likely is a source of satisfaction and stability in your life.

Score: **19-32 Points** – While not an immediate issue, there is opportunity to improve in this area.

Score: **10-18 Points** - This aspect is an issue for you and requires dedicated focus to avoid creating imbalance overall in your life.

Financial Wellness Assessment

The financial aspect of balance involves having an understanding of your financial goals and the short and long-term plans to achieve your financial objectives. Read each statement carefully and respond honestly by using the following scoring:

Strongly Agree	4 Points
Agree	3 Points
Disagree	2 Points
Strongly Disagree	1 Point

	I have a clear understanding of my financial goals and have a healthy view of money.
	I experience little stress when it comes to money or financial matters.
	I balance my financial accounts regularly.
	I know how much debt I currently have.
	I know how much my assets are worth.
	I know my current net worth.
	I know how much money I need to maintain the standard of living that is important to me at the time I retire.
	I have a retirement account and know how the current value of that account.
	I make planning and saving for retirement a financial priority in my life.
	I have a definite plan for retirement and hold myself and my family accountable to that plan.
	Total for Financial Wellness Aspect

Score: **32-40 Points** – This aspect is a great strength for you and most likely is a source of satisfaction and stability in your life.

Score: **19-32 Points** – While not an immediate issue, there is opportunity to improve in this area.

Score: **10-18 Points** - This aspect is an issue for you and requires dedicated focus to avoid creating imbalance overall in your life.

Aspects of Balance Scoring Template

Aspect of Balance	Score
Emotional	
Social	
Spiritual	
Physical	
Intellectual	
Occupational	
Financial	

Balance Wheel Model

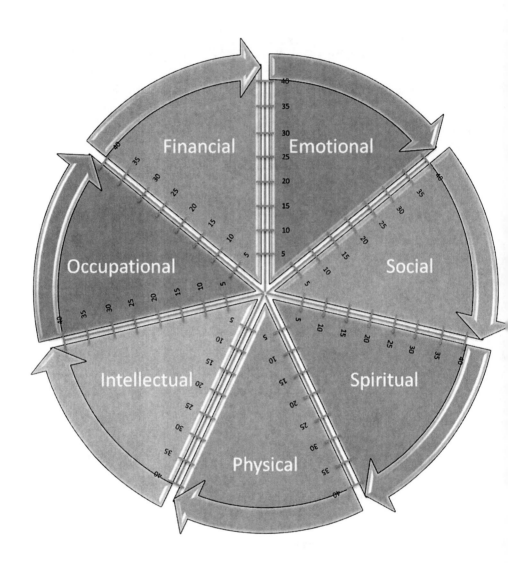

Example of Completed Balance Wheel

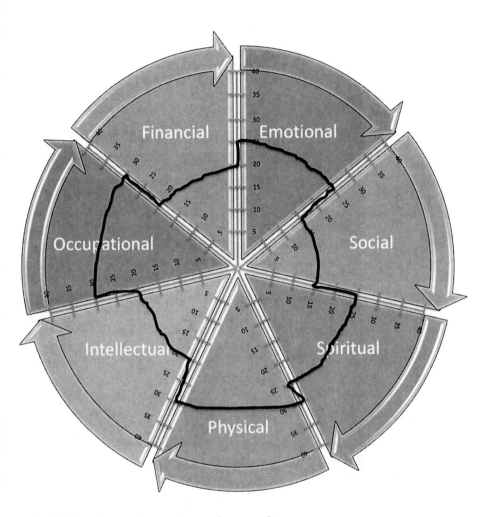

2. What thoughts emerge for you?

3. What are you feelings at this moment?

4. To what degree do you believe this life is "in balance" today?

Aspects of Balance Action Planning Template

Aspect of Balance	Planned Action
_____	1.
	2.
_____	1.
	2.

SMARTS Goals Template

Goal	Actions
Specific	
Measurable	
Action-Oriented	
Realistic	
Time-Bound	
Stretch	

Beginning the Journey to Identifying and Clarifying Purpose:
Creation of Life Mission, Life Vision, Life Values, and Life Purpose Statements

To begin the process of clarifying your purpose, take the next seven days to answer the following questions. These questions, when answered with the appropriate degree of thought and introspection, may not necessarily come easily. I also recommend that during this experience you take the opportunity to journal about what you are thinking, feeling, and experiencing through the process.

This important step will help to provide insight into yourself and can be used in the next section on identifying your passion and understanding your personal "why?"

1. What will be the center of your life?

2. What will be the contribution of your life?

3. What do you want to be known for?

4. What legacy do you want to leave?

5. What would you regret not being able to do in your life?

6. Who inspires you most?

7. How do you define success?

8. How will you know that you are successful?

9. What are you doing when you realize the greatest personal satisfaction and fulfillment?

10. What makes you smile?

11. What do you most enjoy doing in your professional life?

12. What do you most enjoy doing in your personal life?

13. What do you most enjoy doing in your volunteer life?

14. What are the strengths that you have identified in yourself? What are your thoughts about those strengths?

15. What are the strengths that others have identified in you? What are your thoughts about those strengths?

16. What do people typically ask you for help with?

17. If you had to teach something, what would you teach?

18. What are the weaknesses that you have identified in yourself? What are your thoughts about those weaknesses?

19. What are the weaknesses that others have identified in you? What are your thoughts about those weaknesses?

20. What makes you feel great about yourself?

21. Who are the people who are most important in your life?

22. What causes do you strongly and passionately believe in?

23. Where do you spend your time?

24. What are the ten things you most enjoy doing? These are the ten things without which your weeks, months, and years would feel incomplete.

25. If you never had to work another day in your life, how would you spend your time?

26. Where do you spend your money?

27. What values do you hold most dear?

28. How do you define those values?

29. When your life is ending, what will you regret not doing, seeing, or achieving?

By taking the time to fully explore and answer these questions, you will gain insight that will help you to begin crafting your life mission, life vision, life values, and life purpose statements.

Your Life Mission Statement

Your Life Vision Statement

_____

_____

_____

_____

_____

_____

_____

_____

_____

_____

_____

_____

_____

_____

_____

_____

_____

_____

_____

_____

_____

_____

_____

Your Life Values

_____

_____

_____

_____

_____

_____

_____

_____

_____

_____

_____

_____

_____

_____

_____

_____

_____

_____

_____

_____

_____

_____

_____

Below is a list of words that may resonate with you as values for your life. Review the list and circle the ones that are appealing to you.

Accomplishment, Success	Friendship	Privacy
Accountability	Fun	Progress
Accuracy	Generosity	Prosperity, Wealth
Adventure	Gentleness	Punctuality
All for one & one for all	Global view	Quality of work
Beauty	Goodwill	Regularity
Calm, quietude, peace	Goodness	Reliability
Challenge	Gratitude	Resourcefulness
Change	Hard work	Respect for others
Charity	Happiness	Responsiveness
Cleanliness, orderliness	Harmony	Results-oriented
Collaboration	Health	Rule of Law
Commitment	Honor	Safety
Communication	Human-centered	Satisfying others
Community	Improvement	Security
Competence	Independence	Self-givingness
Competition	Individuality	Self-reliance
Concern for others	Inner peace, calm, quietude	Self-thinking
Connection	Innovation	Sensitivity
Content over form	Integrity	Service
Continuous improvement	Intelligence	(to others, society)
Cooperation	Intensity	Simplicity
Coordination	Justice	Skill
Creativity	Kindness	Solving Problems
Customer satisfaction	Knowledge	Speed
Decisiveness	Leadership	Spirit, Spirituality in life
Determination	Love, Romance	Stability
Delight of being, joy	Loyalty	Standardization
Democracy	Maximum utilization	Status
Discipline	(of time, resources)	Strength
Discovery	Meaning	Succeed; A will to-
Diversity	Merit	Success, Achievement
Dynamism	Money	Systemization
Ease of Use	Oneness	Teamwork
Efficiency	Openness	Timeliness
Enjoyment	Other's point of view, inputs	Tolerance
Equality	Patriotism	Tradition
Excellence	Peace, Non-violence	Tranquility
Fairness	Perfection	Trust
Faith	Personal Growth	Truth
Faithfulness	Perseverance	Unity
Family	Pleasure	Variety
Family feeling	Power	Well-being
Flair	Practicality	Wisdom
Freedom, Liberty	Preservation	

From the list that you circled, identify the top ten that you believe are the non-negotiables in your life. Prioritize them in order of importance to you. Then write the top five values in the Your Life Values section on the previous page.

Your Life Purpose Statement

_____

_____

_____

_____

_____

_____

_____

_____

_____

_____

_____

_____

_____

_____

_____

_____

_____

_____

_____

_____

_____

_____

Beginning the Journey to Building and Unleashing Your Passion

Unleashing your passion begins with an understanding of where your emotional energy comes from. Answer the following questions.

1. What is your "why"?

2. What makes your heart beat fast?

3. Where do you gain your energy?

4. What is your greatest motivator?

Beginning the Journey to Establishing a Plan

To begin the thought process behind the establishment of your plan, answer the following questions:

1. With your purpose in mind, what would you be doing differently that would let you know that you are living your purpose?

2. What do you need to begin doing differently today that will allow you to live your purpose?

3. With your life balance assessments in mind, what aspects do you need to focus on developing? What are one or two things that you can be doing differently in those areas that would be better for you?

4. With the end result in mind, what would you want to be saying, doing, thinking, and feeling...

   a. Six months from now?

   b. One year from now?

   c. Three years from now?

   d. Five years from now?

   e. Ten years from now?

5. What do you need to do differently today to allow you to achieve that six-month, one-, three-, five-, and ten-year picture?

6. List your six closest friends. List the top three characteristics of each of these individuals. How do those characteristics align with who you are and where you are going?

7. List your six closest work colleagues. List the top three characteristics of each of these individuals. How do those characteristics align with who you are and where you are going? How will they be a hindrance to you and where you are going?

8. What are the names of the individuals in your life you should be spending more time with because they would be a positive influence on you?

9. What are the names of the individuals in your life you should be spending less time with because they are detracting from you being able to accomplish your goals?

10. What are the names of five individuals you currently do not have a relationship with but who would be valuable to you in providing support in helping you to achieve your goals?

Beginning the Journey to Maintaining Persistence

Persistence in any endeavor is critical. By answering the following questions, you will be able to create a support structure that you can leverage when you face times of opposition, either externally or internally, on your journey to success.

1. Who are three individuals with whom you can share your plans and goals and who will help to hold you accountable?

2. What are some times when you were able to overcome obstacles? What specifically did you do? What did you learn that you could apply in the future?

3. What can you use as your IM to ensure that you stay on track toward the accomplishment of your goals?

4. What consistent and planned time do you need to set aside for personal reflection to identify those needed course corrections? When will you do that? Where will you go to be able to get away by yourself for the time of reflection?

Beginning the Journey to Expressing Gratitude and Celebrating Your Successes

Gratitude is an essential part of success. It brings closure to the current process and allows you to celebrate what has happened and begin to transition to the next season of success. The following questions can help you ensure that you are creating an environment in which you can celebrate your success with full gratitude.

1. What will you do to journal or capture the daily/weekly/ monthly accomplishments that you achieve?

2. Where can you go to get away and reflect?

3. How often can you and should you get away to reflect?

4. Who do you need to include in your time of celebration? Your spouse? Your parents? Your children?

5. What can you do to formally celebrate your successes?

6. Who do you need to contact to tell them what they have done for you and how much you appreciate them?

Your Success Statement

_____
_____
_____
_____
_____
_____
_____
_____
_____
_____
_____
_____
_____
_____
_____
_____
_____
_____
_____
_____
_____
_____
_____

About the Author

I am an architect and catalyst for change, growth, and success.
Dr. Jason Brooks

As a bestselling author, speaker, entrepreneur and executive, leadership consultant, executive coach and co-host of the Step into Leadership Podcast, Dr. Jason Brooks brings a heart for changing lives and growing leaders, one step at a time.

Recognized as one of the most prominent emerging voices in personal and organizational transformation, he is also likely to be one of the most authentic, transparent and "real".

Dr. Brooks is founder and CEO of The Catalyst Leadership Group, a leadership solutions firm located north of Nashville, TN (www.GrowingLeadersNow.com). He is also Chief People Officer with Addiction Campuses, where he serves as a member of the Executive Leadership Team and provides senior-level oversight to the leadership development, organizational effectiveness, strategic planning and human resource initiatives of the company. Prior to joining Addiction Campuses, he held senior executive and leadership roles for American Addiction Centers, Hunt Brothers Pizza/The Britt Hunt Company, LLC. Cracker Barrel Old Country Stores, Inc., Gam, Inc., Accenture, SmithKline Beecham Clinical Laboratories, Emerson Electric Company, and Gaylord Entertainment Company. He has also been engaged as an adjunct faculty member for multiple universities, including Lipscomb University, Liberty University, and Trevecca University. He is a passionate learner and teacher and enjoys investing in the lives of others by developing and leading people on the journey of learning.

Dr. Brooks holds the degrees of doctor of philosophy in psychology, master of business administration, master of science in human services with concentration in mental health counseling, and bachelor of science in management with emphasis in psychology and human resource management. He has achieved certification credentials as a certified executive coach and board-certified coach with specialty designations as an executive, corporate, business, and leadership coach. He is a senior professional in human resources, national certified counselor, and a board-certified Christian counselor, as well as a certified Myers-Briggs Type Indicator facilitator and authorized partner for Everything DiSC.

In an effort to give back to the local community, Dr. Brooks is involved in multiple community organizations in various leadership roles. He is president of Take Another Step Ministries, a Christian faith-based non-profit ministry with a mission to change lives, one step at a time, and lead people to be faith-filled, purpose-focused followers of Christ (www.TakeAnotherStep.org). He also serves in a variety of leadership roles in his local church.

Dr. Brooks lives just north of Nashville, Tennessee, with his bride, Darla, and three wonderful children – two sons and a daughter. Their daughter was adopted from China and came to her "forever family" at nine months old.

When he is not launching and building businesses, consulting, coaching, speaking or writing, Dr. Brooks enjoys spending time with his family and friends. He is an avid photographer and likes to spend time SCUBA diving, reading, teaching and relaxing at the beach.

RESET Resources

You are about to embark on an exciting journey to RESET Your Life! We are here to help. There are multiple resources at your fingertips that will help you on your path and connect you with others who are also committed to living their purpose with passion.

Dr. Jason Brooks Outreach is your home base for tools, tips, and "nuggets of wisdom and inspiration" to assist on your RESET.

On the site you are encouraged to "Connect" with us an "Share your story" as you become part of our growing community.

Connect with us today at
www.DrJasonBrooks.com

Dr. Daddy Life Blog

Check out Dr. Jason's latest motivational and "real life" writings on his personal blog, Dr. Daddy.

Dr. Daddy

www.DrDaddyLife.com

Connect Via Social Media

We invite you to connect with Dr. Jason Brooks via social media on Facebook, LinkedIn, and Twitter at the following addresses:

Facebook
www.facebook.com/drjasonbrooks

LinkedIn
www.linkedin.com/in/jasontbrooks

Twitter
www.twitter.com/drjasonbrooks

The
Catalyst Leadership Group
Growing high-impact leaders from the "inside-out"

The Catalyst Leadership Group's mission is to grow high- impact leaders from the "inside-out" and help them to unleash their full potential to deliver high-impact results through their work and leave a legacy of success and significance in life.

We are uniquely positioned to accomplish our vision to align, engage, grow and inspire high-impact leaders through bringing expertise and solutions in four key areas...

Leadership Consulting
Leader and Executive Coaching
Personal and Leadership Assessments
Professional Speaking

www.GrowingLeadersNow.com
615.777.6240

CPSIA information can be obtained
at www.ICGtesting.com
Printed in the USA
FFOW01n1453120217
32267FF

9 780615 728124